HOW TO DRAW ANYTHING:

300 DRAWINGS OF ADORABLE THINGS, ANIMALS, FOOD, GIFTS, AND OTHER AMAZING ITEMS | BOOK FOR KIDS

ISBN: 979-8871554906

HOW TO USE THIS BOOK

PENCILS AND ERASER

GET YOUR SHARP PENCIL AND TRUSTED ERASER SET FOR A SMOOTH DRAWING EXPERIENCE. IF YOU WANT TO ADD A DASH OF COLOR TO YOUR CREATION, COLORED PENCILS ARE YOUR BEST CHOICE.

4-STEP EXAMPLE OF HOW TO DRAW

WHEN DRAWING WITH YOUR PENCIL, USE GENTLE LINES TO KEEP THE SKETCH CLEAN AND MAKE CORRECTING MISTAKES EASIER. TRACE LIGHTLY AND FOLLOW THE ARROWS TO FINISH YOUR PIECE. AFTERWARDS, USE THE BLANK SPACE TO EXPERIMENT AND PERFECT YOUR DRAWING SKILLS ON YOUR OWN.

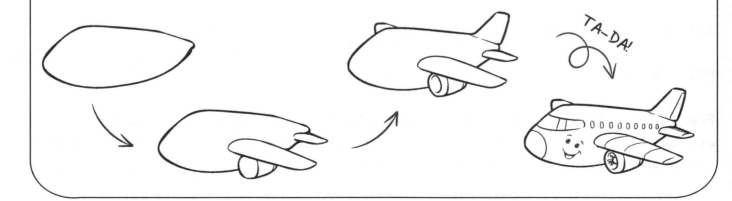

CONTENTS

TOYS AND SPORTS

FOOD AND KITCHEN ITEMS

BURGER 34
ICE CREAM 34
FRIED EGG 34
MUFFIN 35
HOT DOG 35
SANDWICH 35
PIZZA 36
TACO 36
FRENCH FRIES 36
BREAD 37
DONUT 37
POPSICLE 37
COOKIE 38
CUPCAKE 38
BIRTHDAY CAKE 38
CROISSANT 39
PANCAKES 39
POPCORN 39
BURRITO 40
CHIPS 40
SOUP 40
YOGURT 41
JAM 41
PORRIDGE 41
MARSHMALLOW 42
CHICKEN DRUMSTICK 42

SAUSAGES 42
KETCHUP 43
FRIED BACON 43
BUTTER 43
SWISS CHEESE 44
WHIPPED CREAM 44
CANDY 44
GINGERBREAD 45
PIE 45
CAKE 45
DELI HAM 46
SALAMI 46
MEAT CHOP 46
FRENCH BAGUETTE 47
ROASTED TURKEY 47
CHOCOLATE 47
PRETZEL 48
NOODLES 48
MEAT 48
SUSHI 49
BOILED EGG 49
CHALLAH BREAD 49
HONEY 50
TEA BAG 50
COOKING OIL 50
WATER BOTTLE 51

ORANGE JUICE 51
SMOOTHIE 51
LEMONADE 52
MILK 52
HOT CHOCOLATE 52
OVEN GLOVE 53
CHEF HAT 53
APRON 53
SAUCE 54
KNIFE 54
PICNIC BAG 54
FRYING PAN 55
HAND MIXER 55
IMMERSION BLENDER 55
TONGS 56
GRATER 56
LADLE 56
POT 57
PITCHER 57
OVEN 57
KETTLE 58
TOASTER 58
MICROWAVE 58
FOOD PROCESSOR 59
WHISK 59
PEELER 59

FRUIT, VEGETABLE AND PLANTS

STRAWBERRY 61
GRAPES 61
APPLE 61
CHERRIES 62
BANANA 62
PUMPKIN 62
ORANGE 63
PEAR 63
BLACK CURRANT 63
PINEAPPLE 64
CANTALOUPE 64
PEACH 64
WATERMELON 65
PERSIMMON 65
MEDLAR 65
LEMON 66
MANGO 66
FIG 66
MELON 67
PAPAYA 67
PASSION FRUIT 67
PLUM 68
POMEGRANATE 68
QUINCE 68
ACKEE 69

APRICOT 69
KIWI 69
RASPBERRY 70
OLIVES 70
AVOCADO 70
COCONUT 71
HAZELNUT 71
PEANUT 71
CASHEWS 72
ALMONDS 72
PISTACHIOS 72
TOMATO 73
MUSHROOM 73
CARROT 73
RADISH 74
BROCCOLI 74
GARLIC BULB 74
ONION 75
LETTUCE 75
EGGPLANT 75
POTATOES 76
BELL PEPPER 76
KOHLRABI 76
ASPARAGUS 77
LEEK 77

DAIKON 77
PEAS 78
CHILI PEPPER 78
ZUCCHINI 78
CORN 79
ARTICHOKE 79
CAULIFLOWER 79
GINGER 80
CUCUMBERS 80
SWEET POTATO 80
ACORN 81
FENNEL 81
BUTTERNUT SQUASH 81
CACTUS 82
TREE 82
LEAF 82
HOLLY 83
CHRISTMAS TREE 83
FLOWER 83
PALM TREE 84
TULIP 84
BOUQUET 84
BELLFLOWER 85
GRASS BUSH 85
WILLOW BRANCH 85

ANIMALS AND EVERYDAY THINGS

DOG 87
DINOSAUR 87
CHICK 87
BEAR 88
BEE 88
RABBIT 88
TIGER 89
RACCOON 89
MONKEY 89
SQUID 90
PENGUIN 90
SHEEP 90
GIRAFFE 91
SQUIRREL 91
ZEBRA 91
FOX 92
POLAR BEAR 92
KOALA 92
LADYBUG 93
EAGLE 93
PIG 93
IGUANA 94
LEOPARD 94
HEDGEHOG 94

FISH 95
SCORPION 95
HIPPO 95
KANGAROO 96
RHINO 96
NARWHAL 96
TURTLE 97
CENTIPEDE 97
SHARK 97
MOUSE 98
PUPPY 98
FROG 98
HORSE 99
DUCK 99
WHALE 99
CROCODILE 100
OWL 100
ELEPHANT 100
CAT 101
HAMSTER 101
PANDA 101
DOLPHIN 102
JELLYFISH 102
SEAL 102

SNAKE 103
BUNNY 103
BUTTERFLY 103
HYENA 104
ALLIGATOR 104
PLATYPUS 104
SUN 105
RAINBOW 105
JERRYCAN 105
TOILET PAPER 106
LAPTOP 106
BOOK 106
CANDLE 107
SCREWDRIVER 107
SAFETY HELMET 107
PLIERS 108
PENCIL 108
TRAFFIC CONE 108
SCREW 109
GIFT 109
DIAMOND 109
UMBRELLA 110
TELEPHONE 110
MOON 110

TOYS AND SPORTS

ROCKET

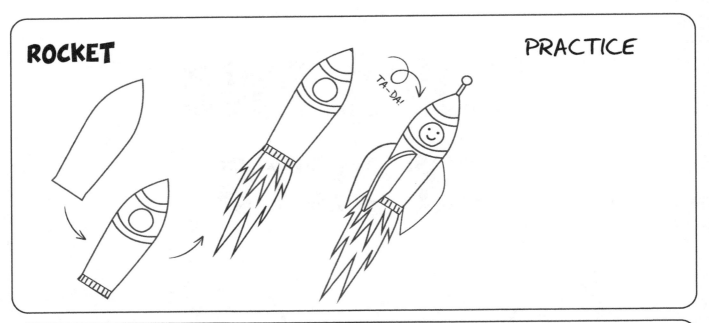

DRUM

BLOCKS

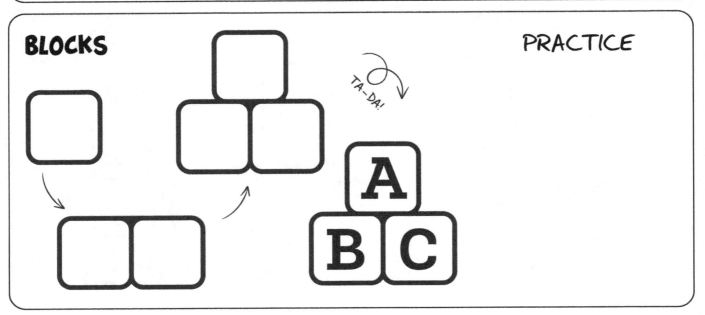

TRAIN

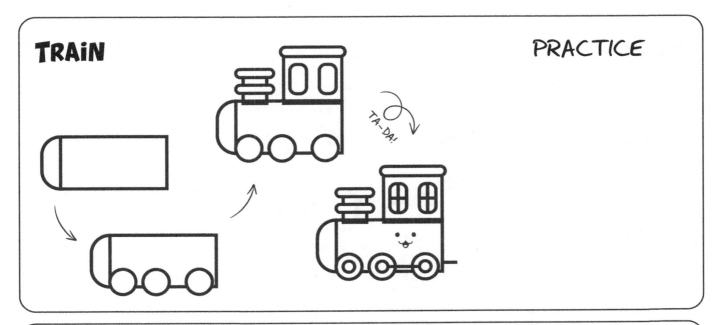

BASKETBALL

PINWHEEL

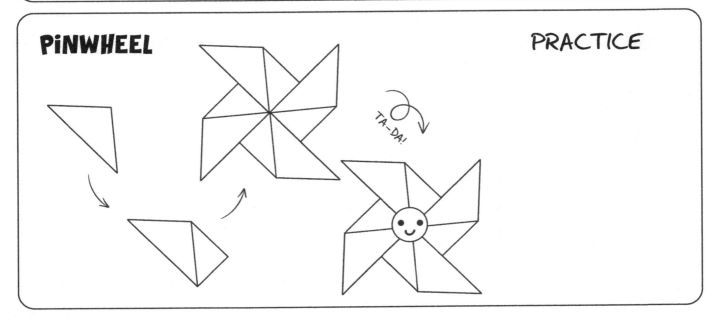

TANK

TA-DA!

STACKING

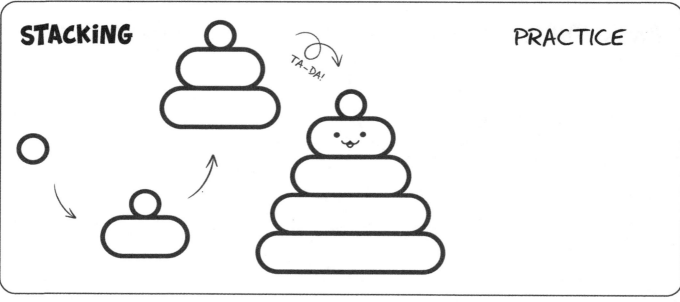

TA-DA!

RUBBER DUCK

TA-DA!

TRUCK

BOAT

SPINNING TOP

SHIP

AIRPLANE

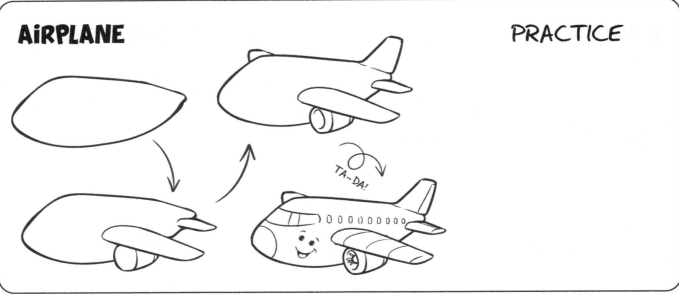

BALLOON

PALETTE

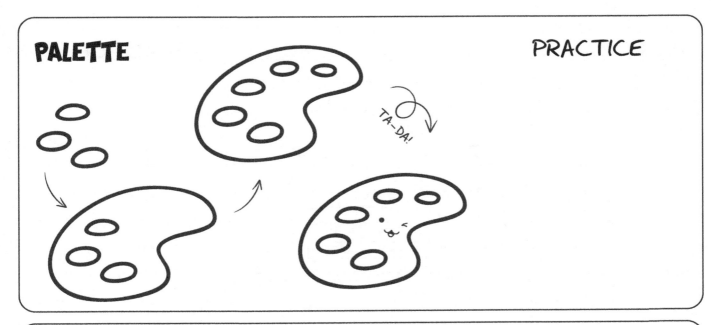

SEESAW

HOUSE

BUS

TA-DA!

ORIGAMI

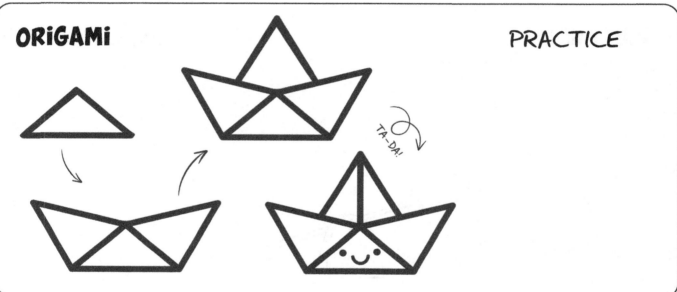

TA-DA!

ELECTRONIC PIANO

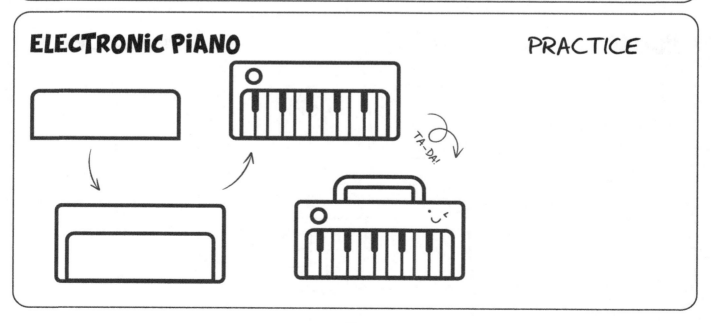

TA-DA!

AiR BALLOON

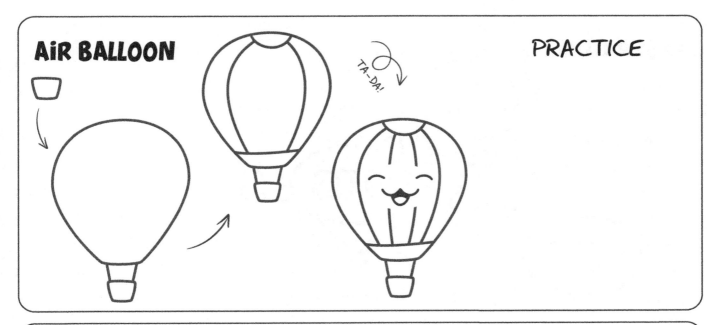

TA-DA!

BUNNY TOY

TA-DA!

MARACAS

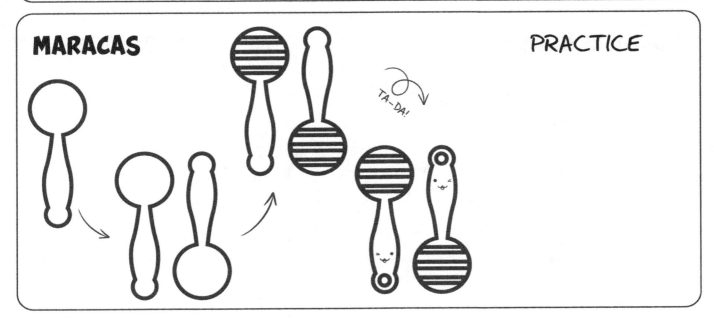

TA-DA!

LASER GUN

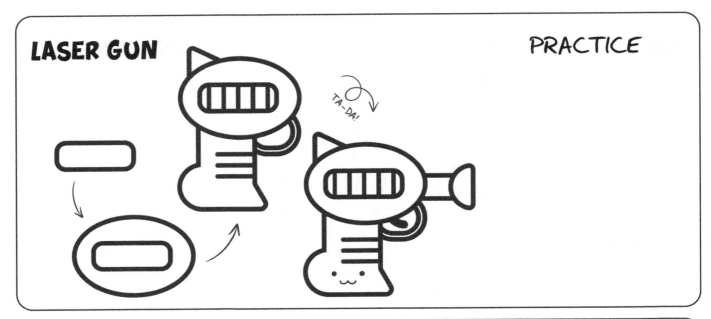

SUBMARINE

ROCKING HORSE

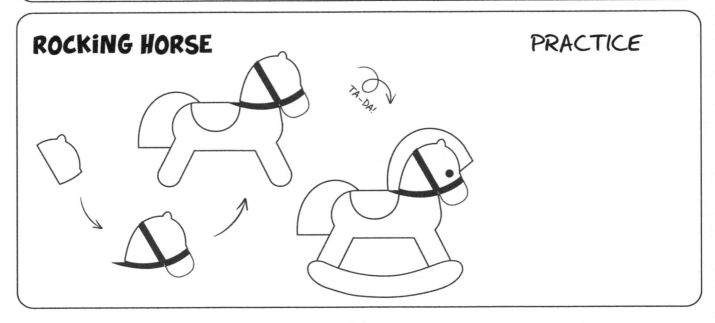

CASTLE

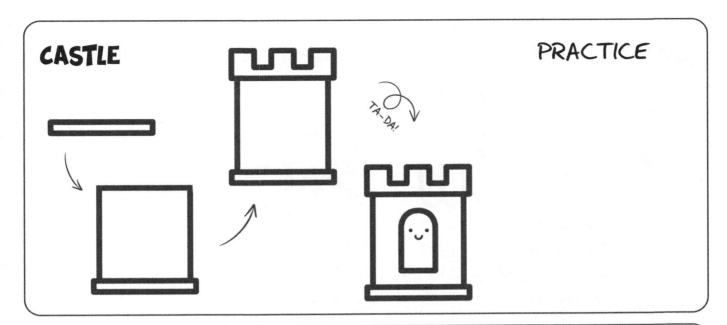

TA-DA!

CAR

TA-DA!

JACK IN THE BOX

TA-DA!

GIRL

TA-DA!

TEDDY BEAR

TA-DA!

KITE

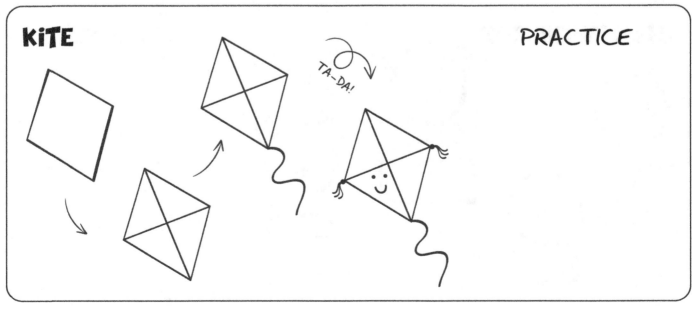

TA-DA!

MUSIC BOX

PAPER AIRPLANE

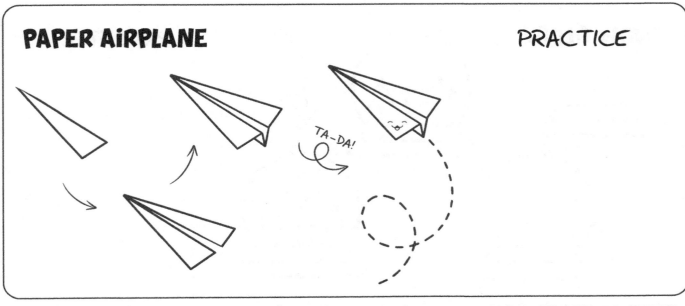

RATTLE DRUM

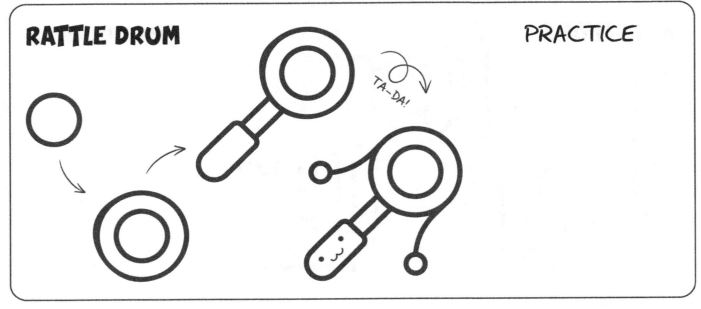

SAND BUCKET

TA-DA!

SNOW GLOBE

TA-DA!

XYLOPHONE

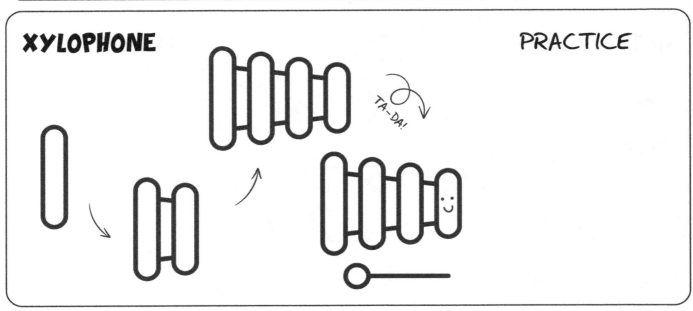

TA-DA!

SCOOTER

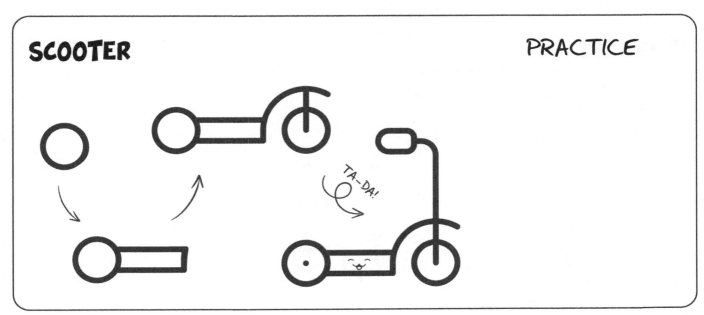

NUTCRACKER

UFO

KARAOKE

TA-DA!

SLINGSHOT

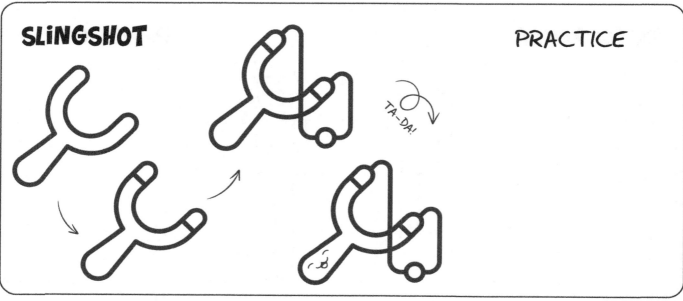

TA-DA!

GAMEBOY

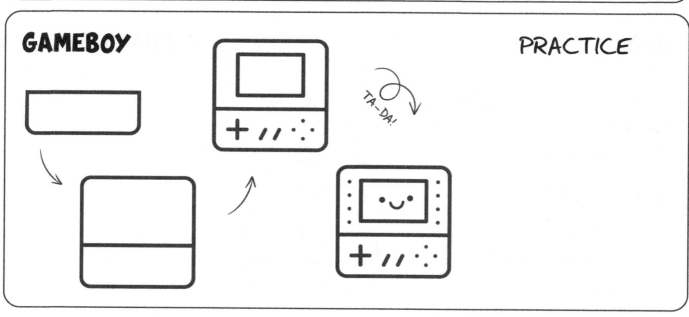

TA-DA!

SOLDIER

GAMEPAD

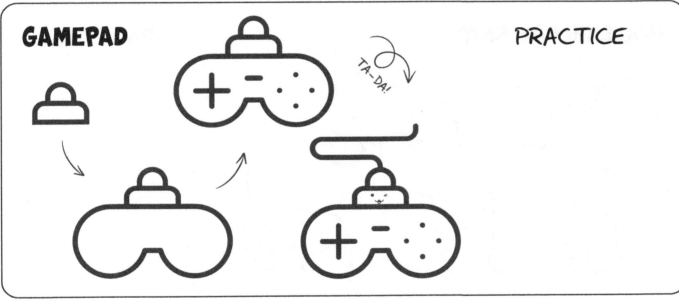

SPINNER

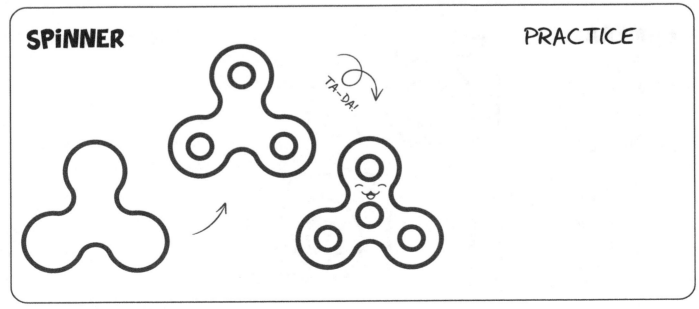

SKATEBOARD

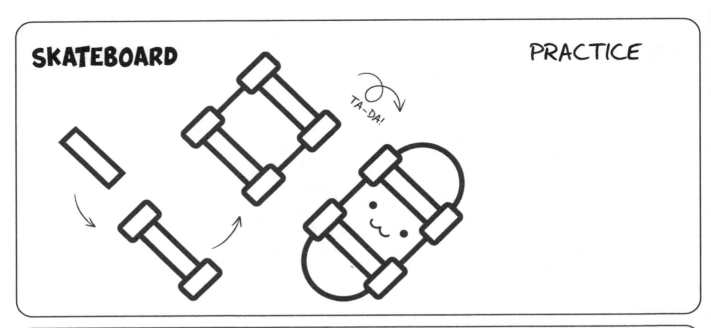

TA-DA!

ROLLERBLADE SKATES

TA-DA!

CAMERA

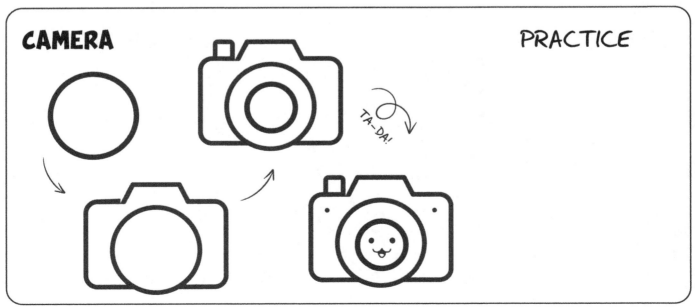

TA-DA!

WATER GUN

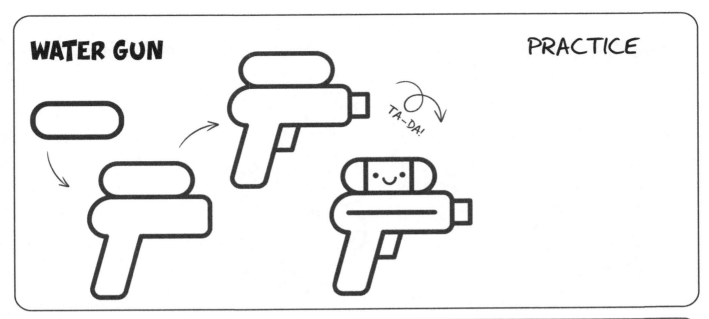

PARACHUTE

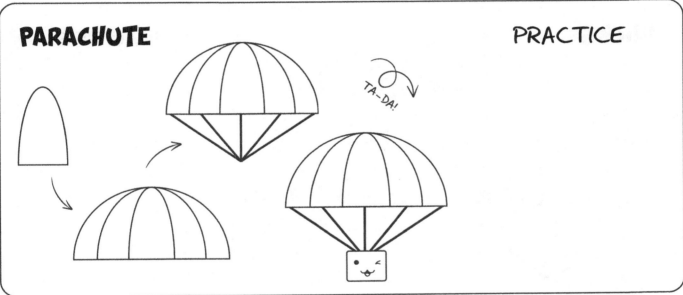

WALKIE TALKIE

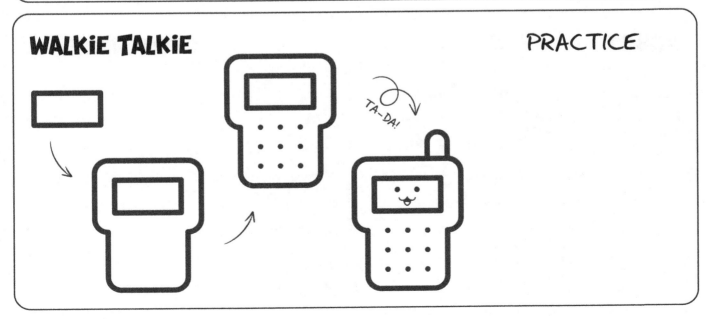

PUZZLE PIECE

TA-DA!

BRICKS

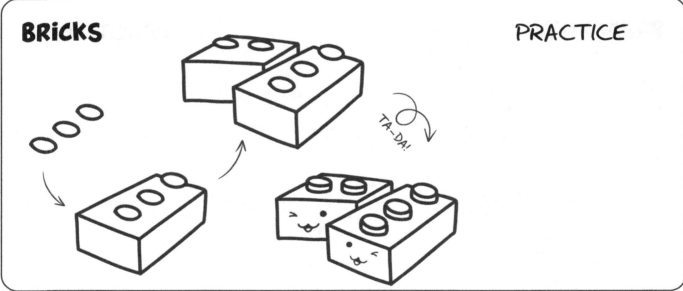

TA-DA!

ROBOT

TA-DA!

CROWN PRACTICE

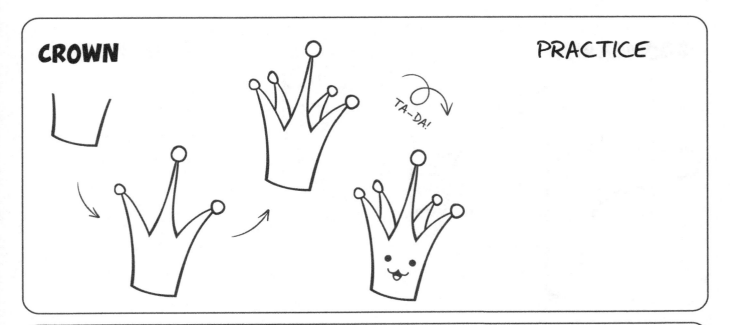

HELMET PRACTICE

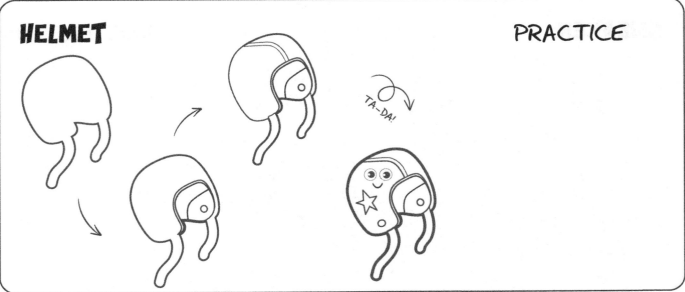

TARGET PRACTICE

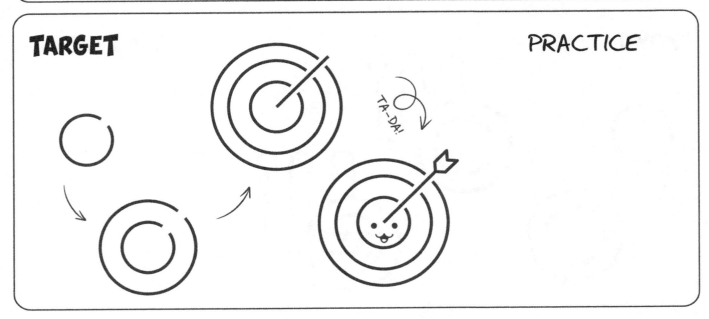

27

BOOMERANG

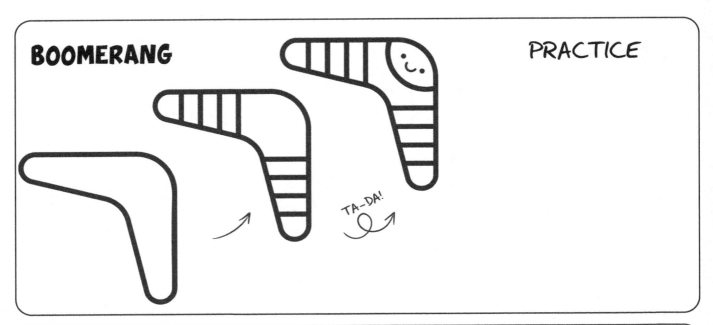

TA-DA!

SNEAKER

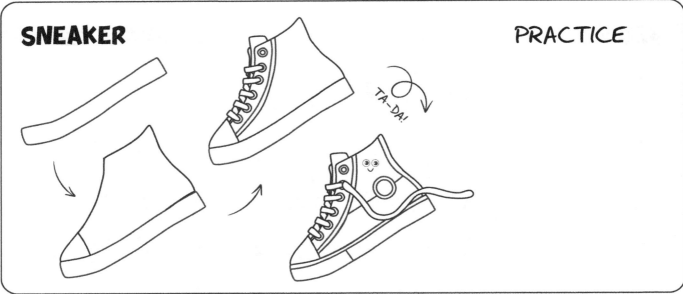

TA-DA!

YOYO

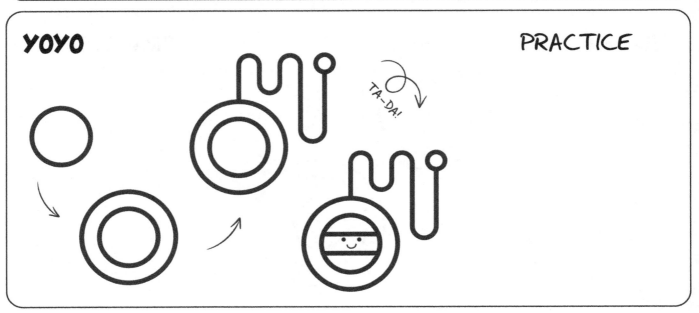

TA-DA!

WHISTLE

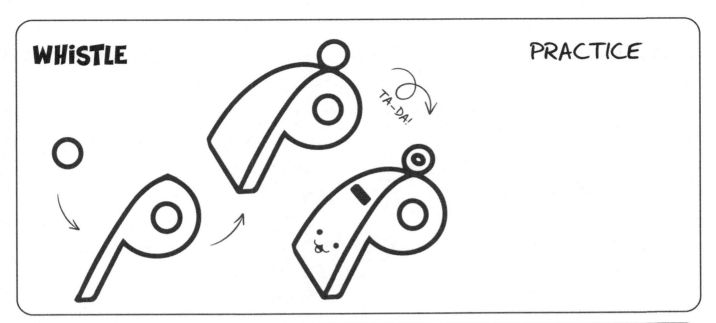

BICYCLE

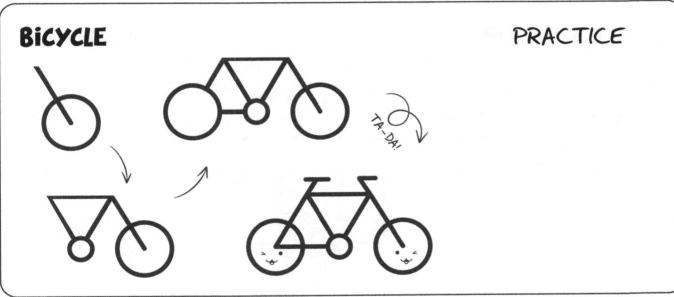

TROPHY

BiRDiE

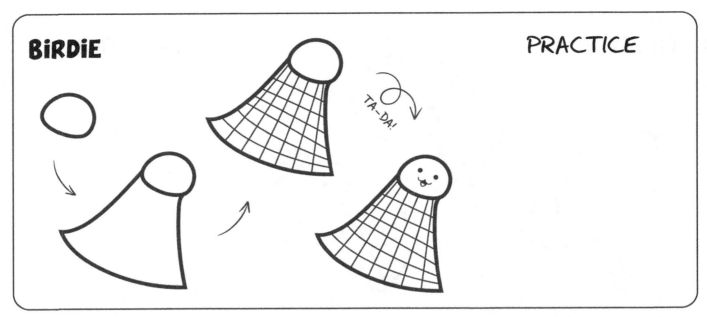

TA-DA!

BACKBOARD RiM

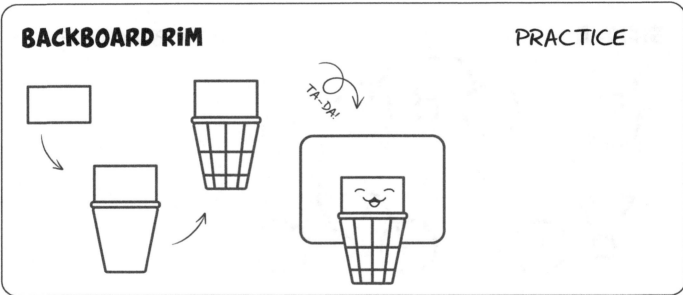

TA-DA!

POGO STiCK

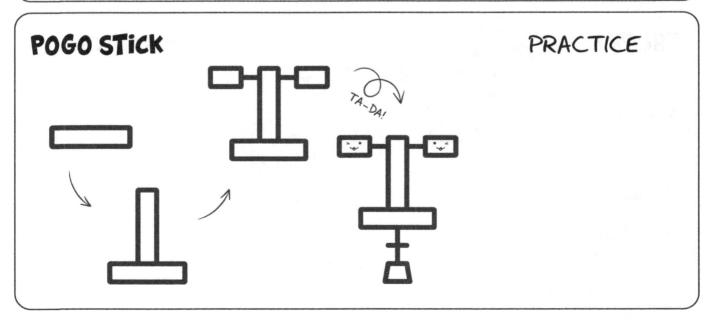

TA-DA!

SWORD

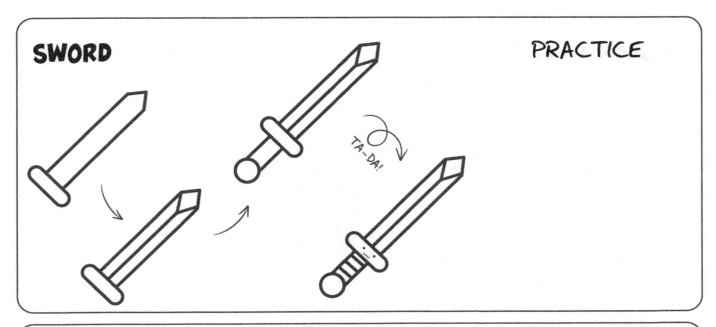

TENNIS RACKET

BASEBALL BATS

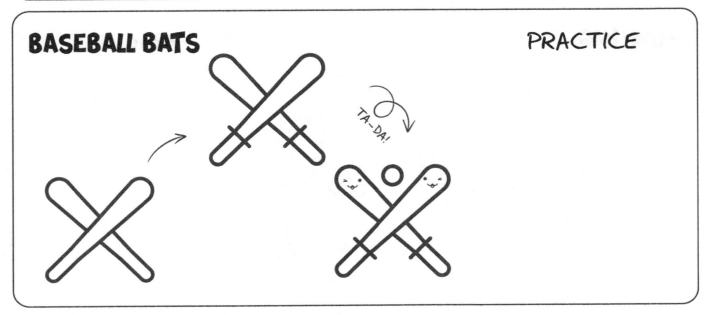

BASEBALL GLOVE

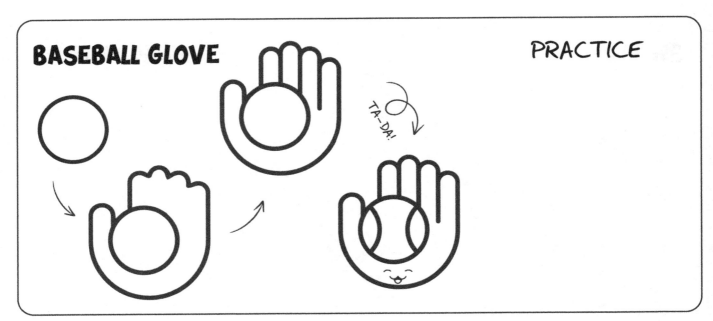

TA-DA!

WEIGHTS

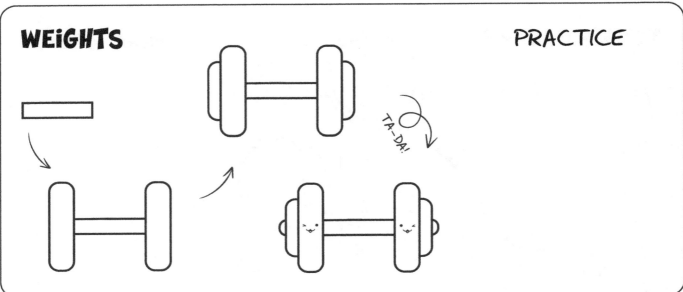

TA-DA!

BOWLING

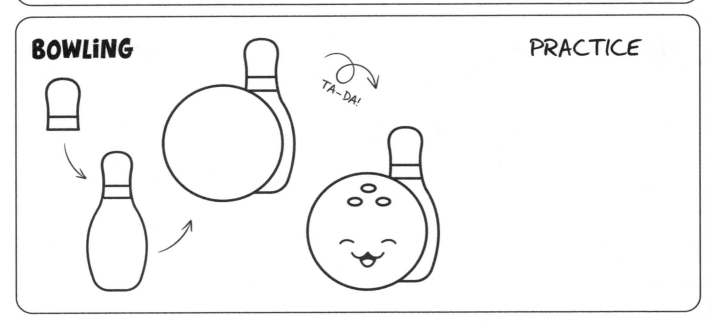

TA-DA!

FOOD AND KITCHEN iTEMS

BURGER

TA-DA!

iCE CREAM

TA-DA!

FRiED EGG

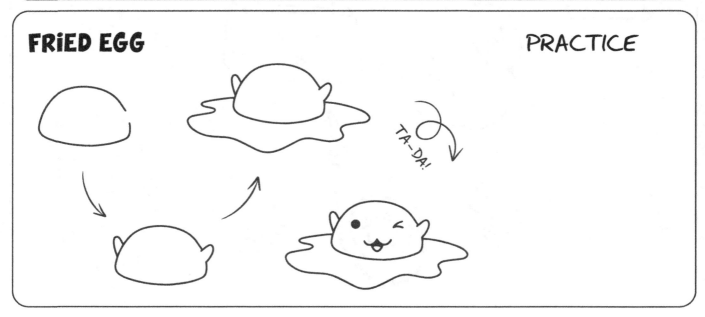

TA-DA!

MUFFIN

TA-DA!

HOT DOG

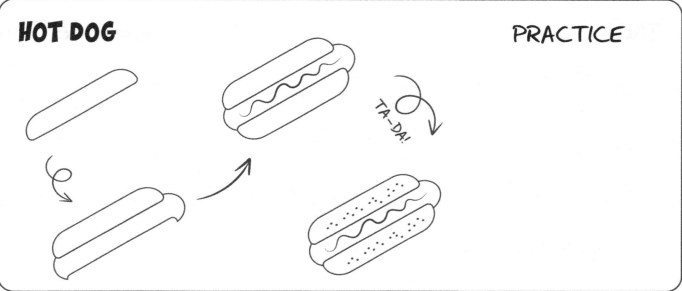

TA-DA!

SANDWICH

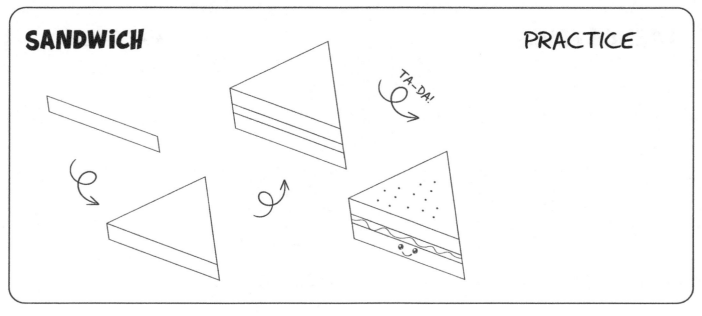

TA-DA!

PiZZA

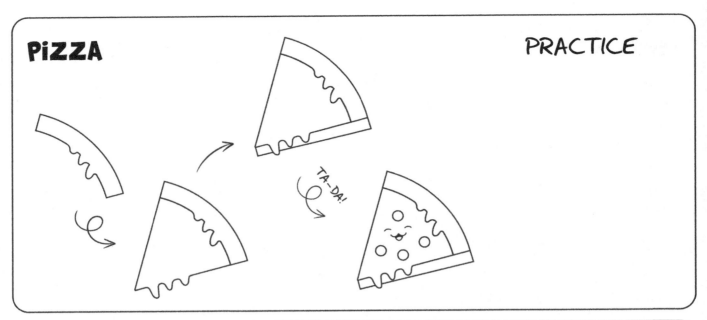

TA-DA!

TACO

TA-DA!

FRENCH FRiES

TA-DA!

BREAD

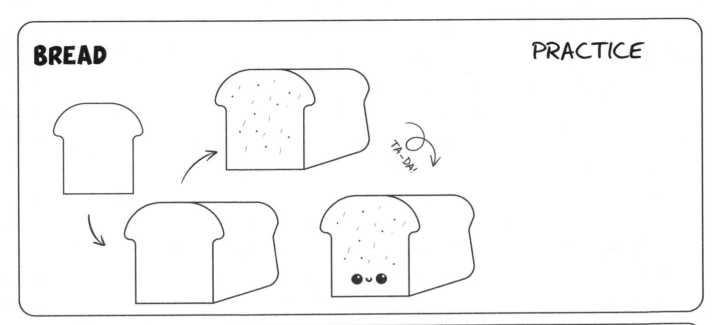

TA-DA!

DONUT

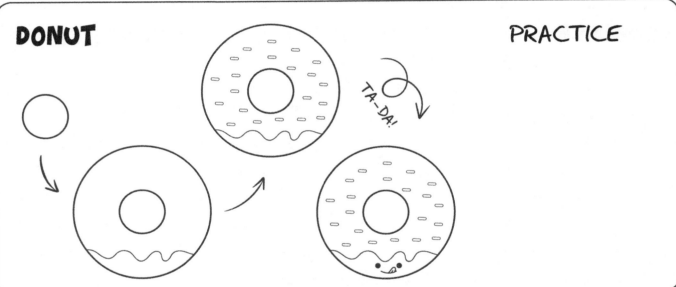

TA-DA!

POPSICLE

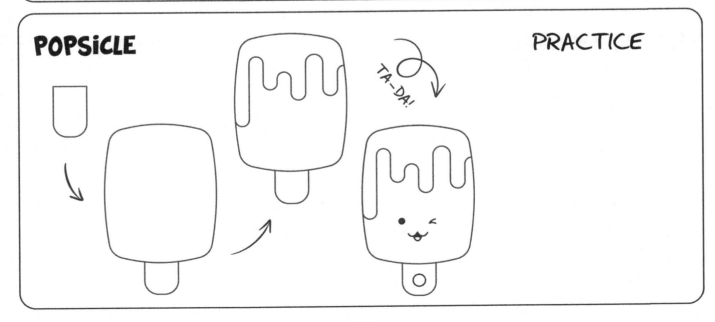

TA-DA!

COOKIE

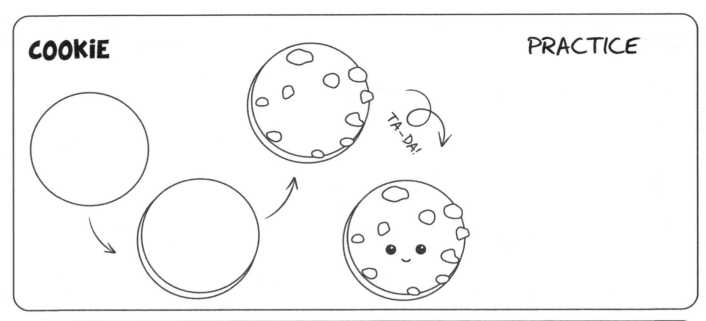

TA-DA!

CUPCAKE

TA-DA!

BIRTHDAY CAKE

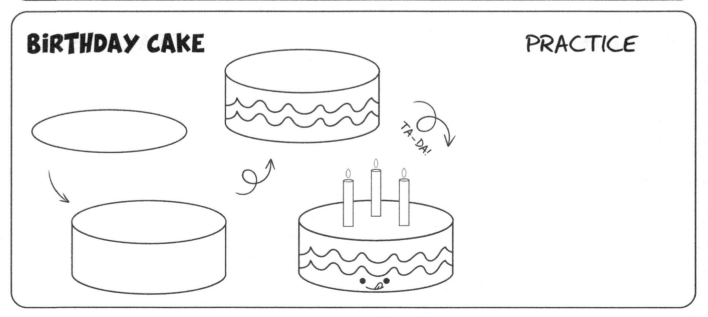

TA-DA!

CROISSANT

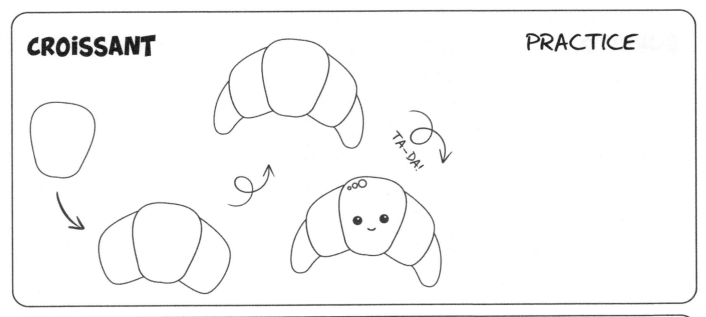

TA-DA!

PANCAKES

TA-DA!

POPCORN

TA-DA!

BURRITO 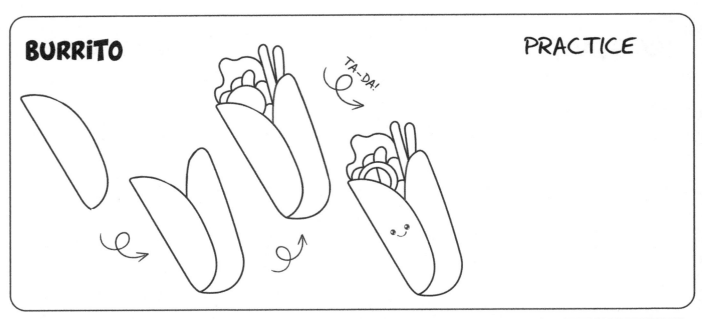 PRACTICE

CHIPS 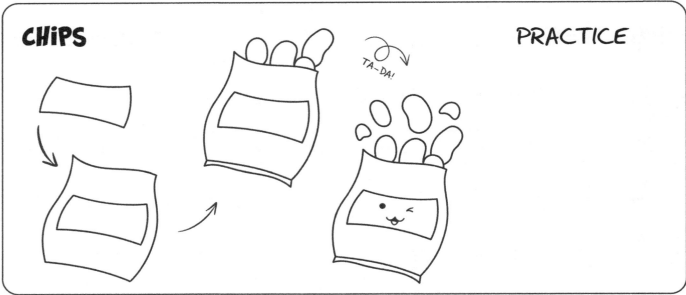 PRACTICE

SOUP 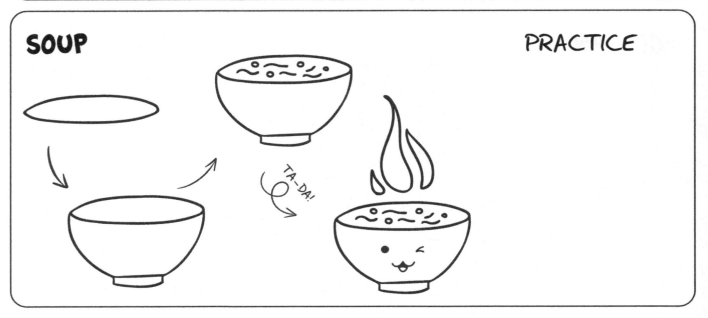 PRACTICE

YOGURT

TA-DA!

JAM

TA-DA!

PORRIDGE

TA-DA!

MARSHMALLOW

TA-DA!

CHICKEN DRUMSTICK

TA-DA!

SAUSAGES

TA-DA!

KETCHUP

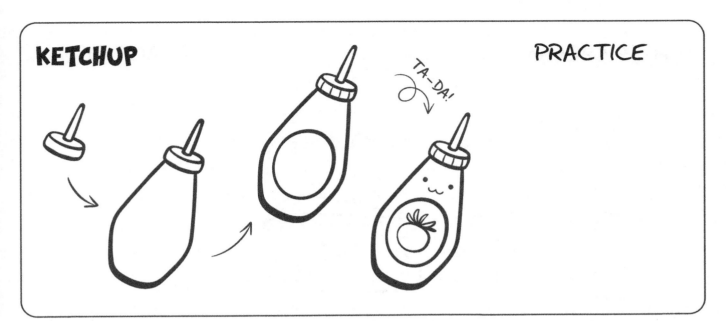

FRIED BACON

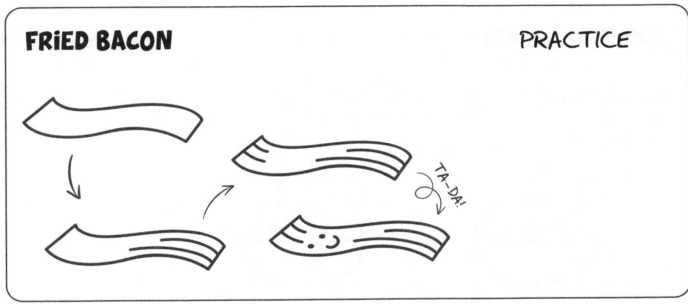

BUTTER

SWISS CHEESE

WHIPPED CREAM

CANDY

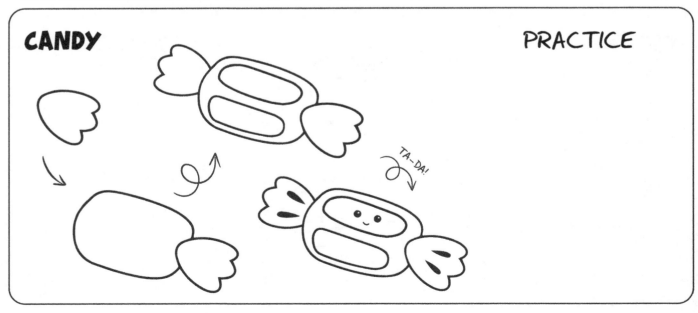

GINGERBREAD

TA-DA!

PIE

TA-DA!

CAKE

TA-DA!

DELI HAM

SALAMI

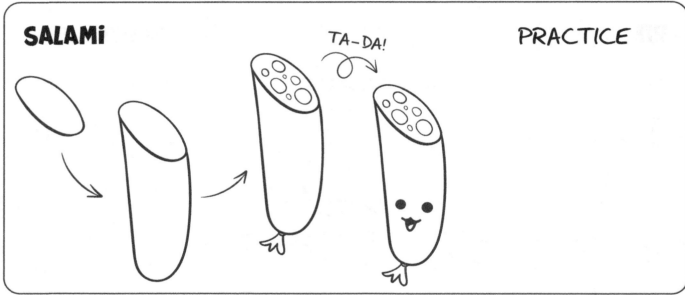

MEAT CHOP

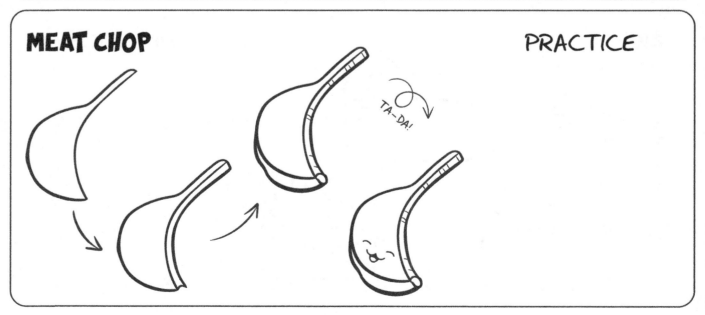

FRENCH BAGUETTE

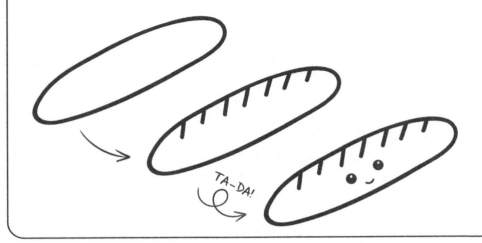

TA-DA!

ROASTED TURKEY

TA-DA!

CHOCOLATE

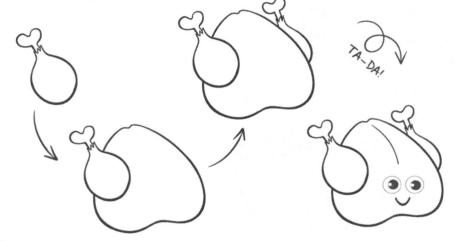

TA-DA!

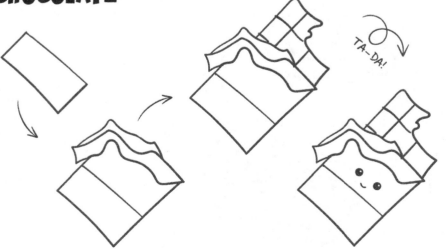

PRETZEL

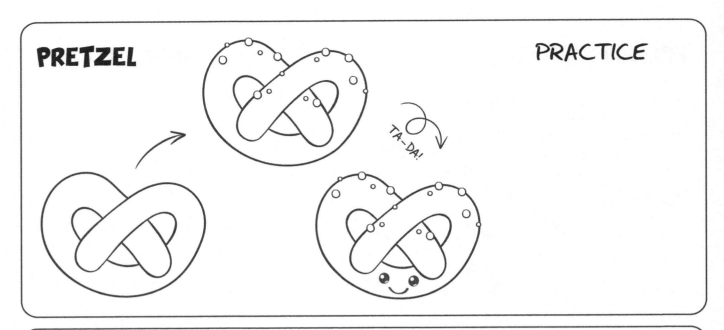

TA-DA!

NOODLES

TA-DA!

MEAT

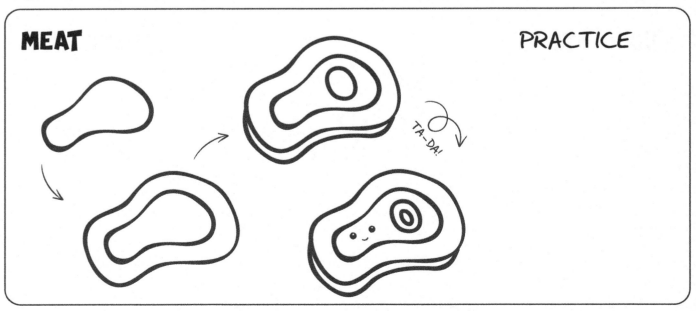

TA-DA!

SUSHI PRACTICE

BOILED EGG PRACTICE

CHALLAH BREAD PRACTICE

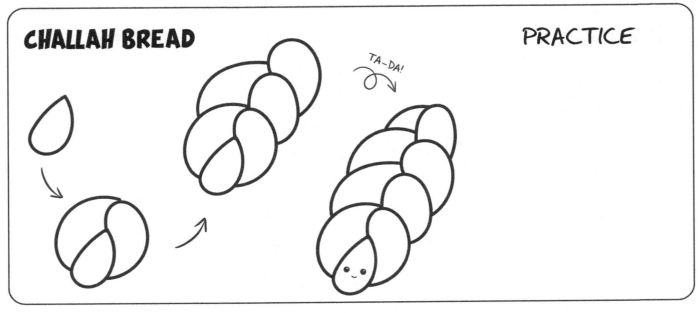

HONEY

TA-DA!

TEA BAG

TA-DA!

COOKING OIL

TA-DA!

COOKING OIL

WATER BOTTLE

ORANGE JUICE

SMOOTHIE

LEMONADE

MILK

HOT CHOCOLATE

OVEN GLOVE

TA-DA!

CHEF HAT

TA-DA!

APRON

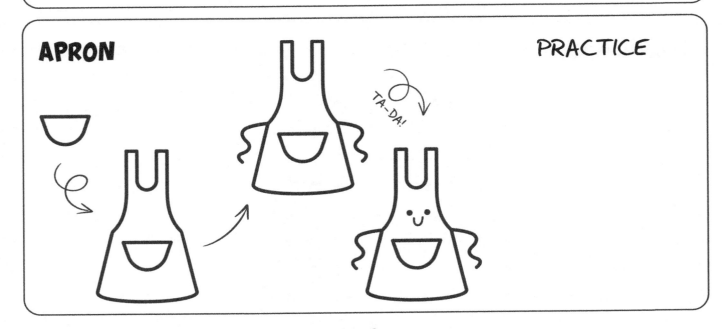

TA-DA!

SAUCE

KNIFE

PICNIC BAG

FRYING PAN

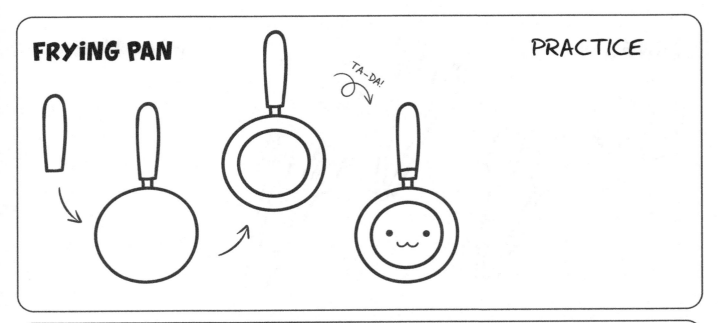

TA-DA!

HAND MIXER

TA-DA!

IMMERSION BLENDER

TA-DA!

TONGS

TA-DA!

GRATER

TA-DA!

LADLE

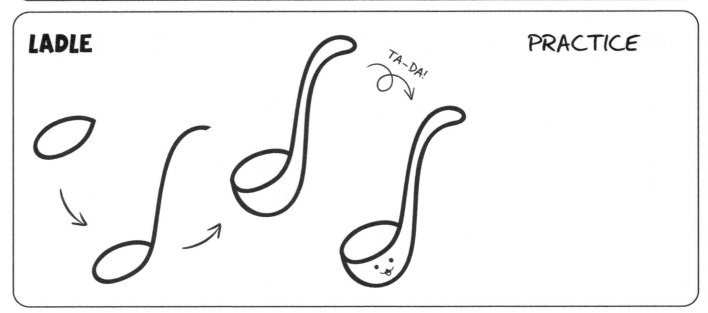

TA-DA!

POT

PITCHER

OVEN

KETTLE

TA-DA!

TOASTER

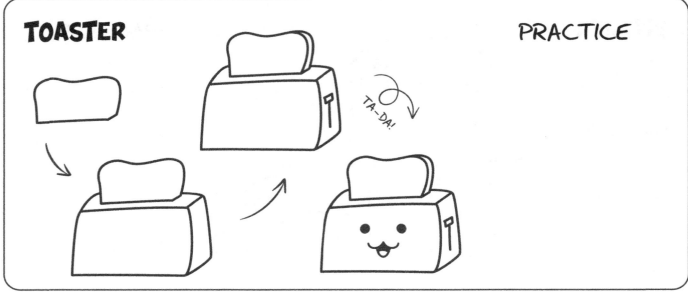

TA-DA!

MICROWAVE

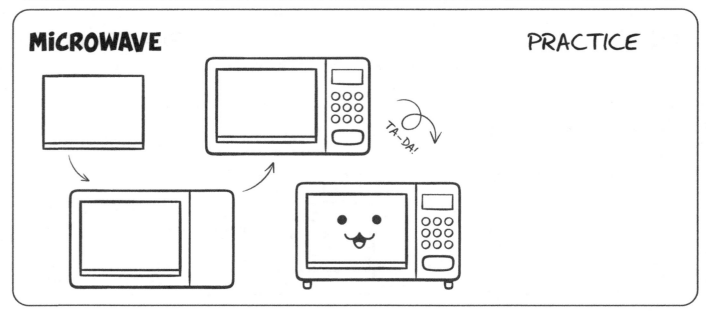

TA-DA!

FOOD PROCESSOR

TA-DA!

WHISK

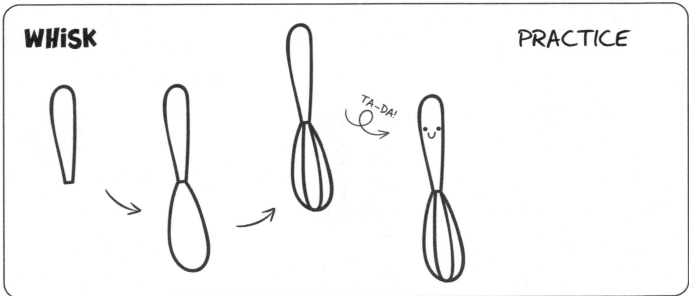

TA-DA!

PEELER

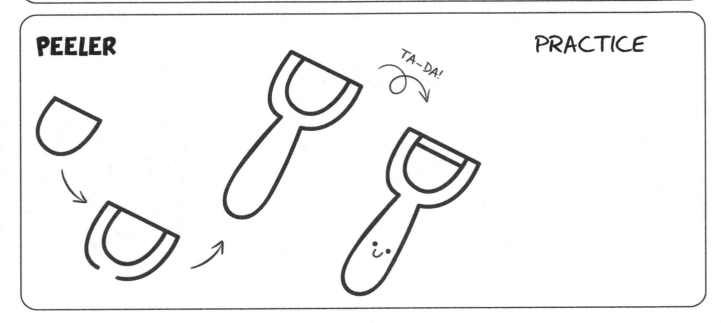

TA-DA!

FRUIT, VEGETABLE, AND PLANTS

STRAWBERRY PRACTICE

GRAPES PRACTICE

APPLE PRACTICE

CHERRIES

TA-DA!

BANANA

TA-DA!

PUMPKIN

TA-DA!

ORANGE

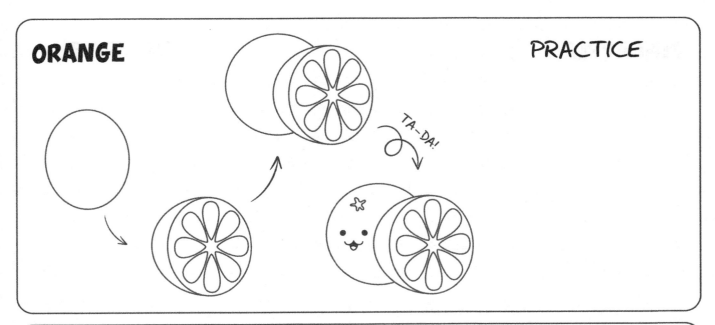

TA-DA!

PEAR

TA-DA!

BLACK CURRANT

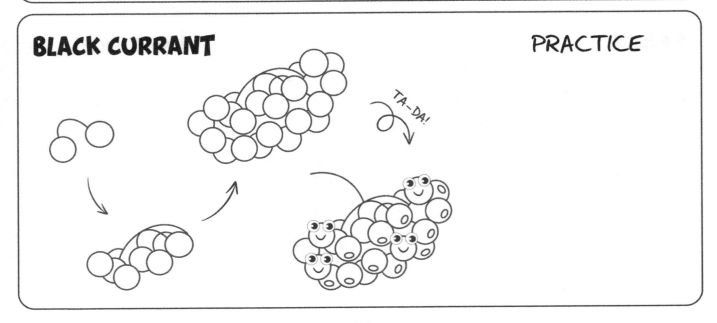

TA-DA!

PINEAPPLE

CANTALOUPE

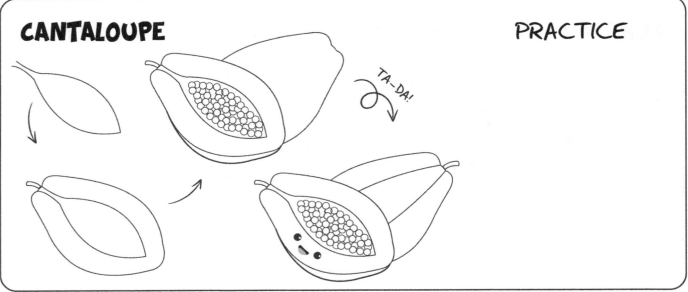

PEACH

WATERMELON

TA-DA!

PERSIMMON

TA-DA!

MEDLAR

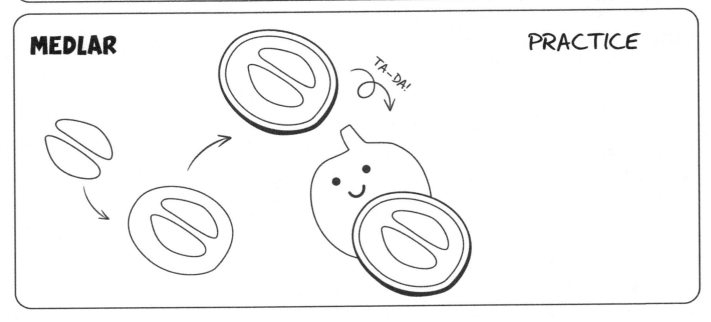

TA-DA!

LEMON

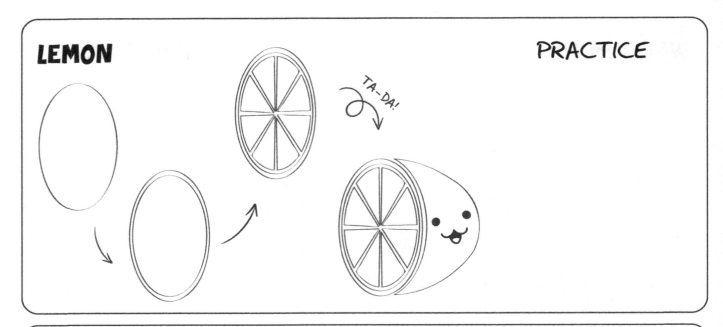

TA-DA!

MANGO

TA-DA!

FIG

TA-DA!

MELON

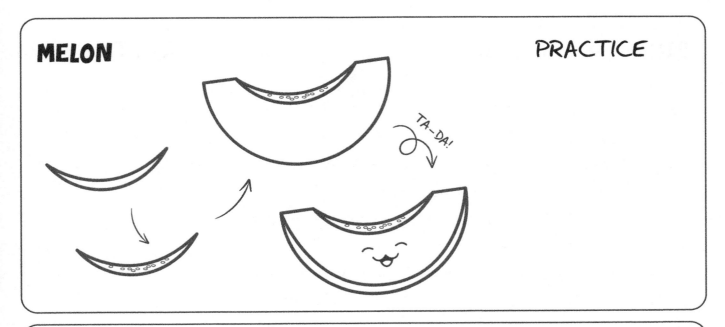

PAPAYA

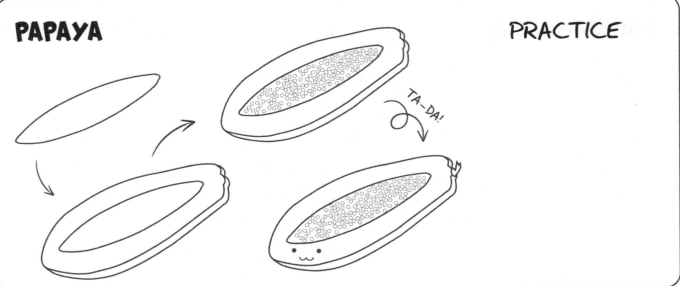

PASSION FRUIT

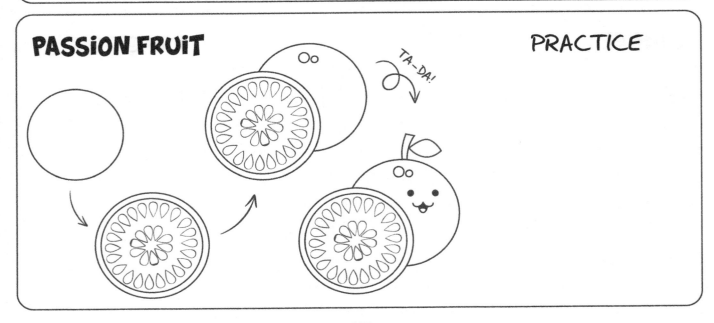

PLUM

TA-DA!

POMEGRANATE

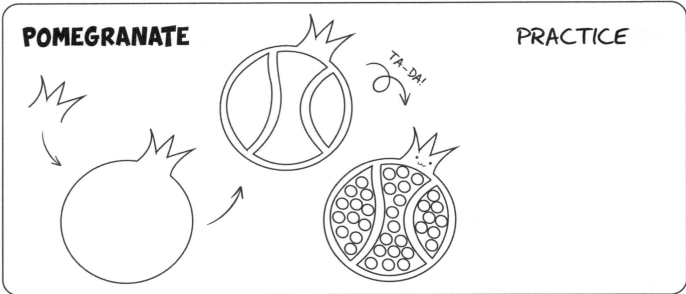

TA-DA!

QUINCE

TA-DA!

ACKEE

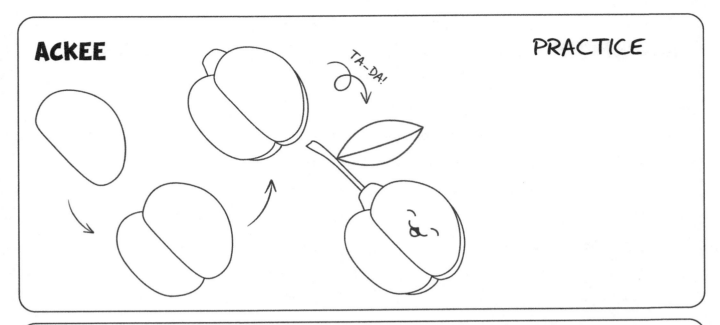

TA-DA!

APRICOT

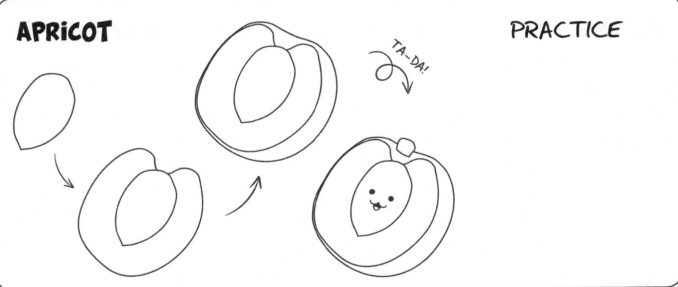

TA-DA!

KiWi

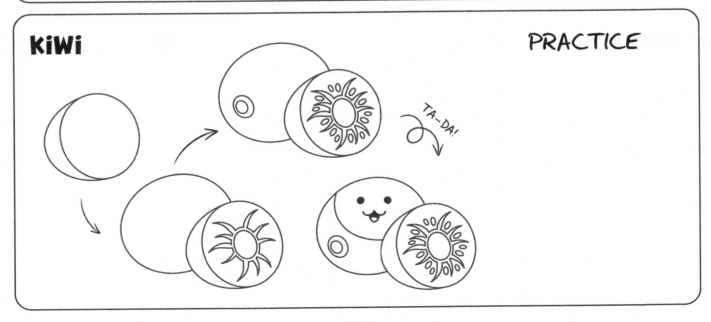

TA-DA!

RASPBERRY

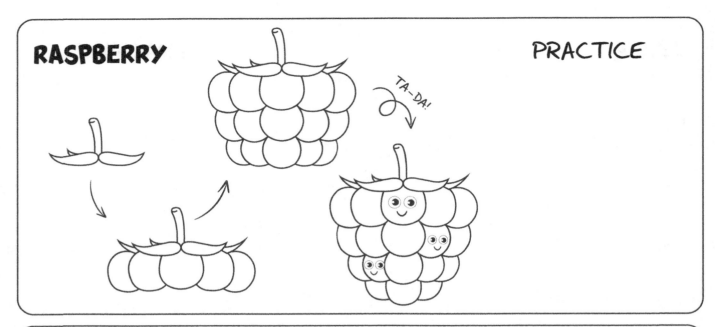

TA-DA!

OLIVES

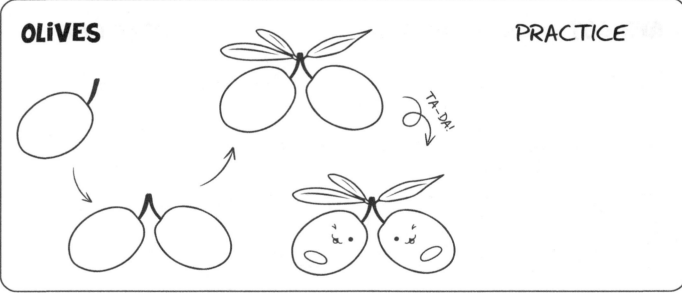

TA-DA!

AVOCADO

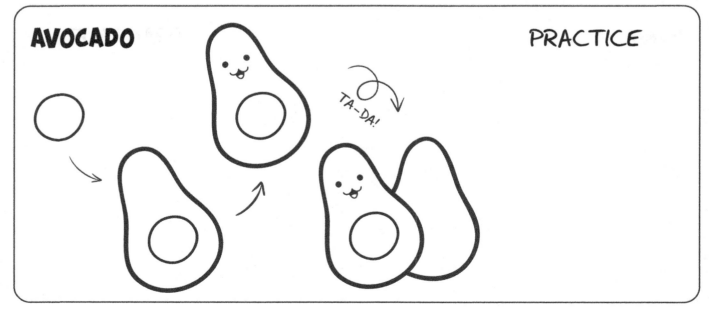

TA-DA!

COCONUT

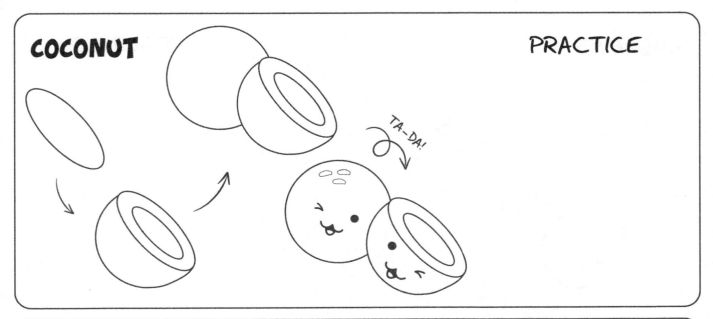

HAZELNUT

PEANUT

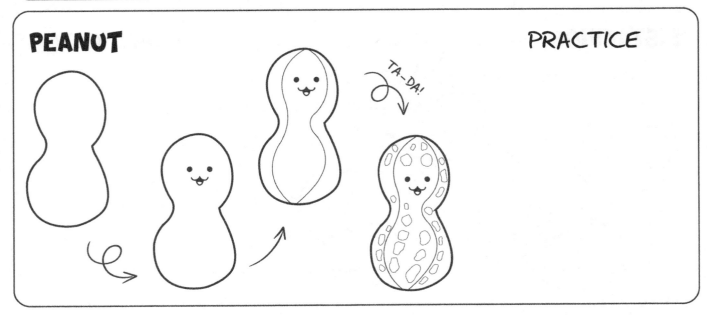

CASHEWS

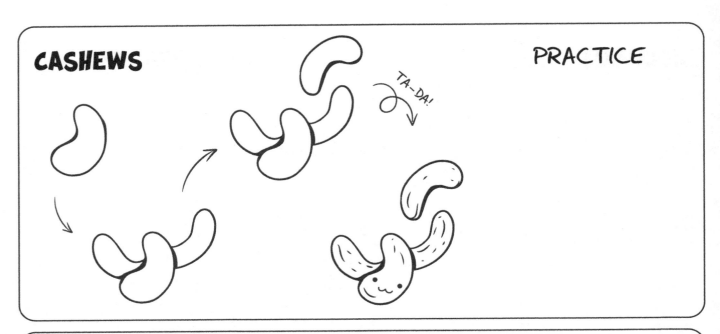

TA-DA!

ALMONDS

TA-DA!

PISTACHIOS

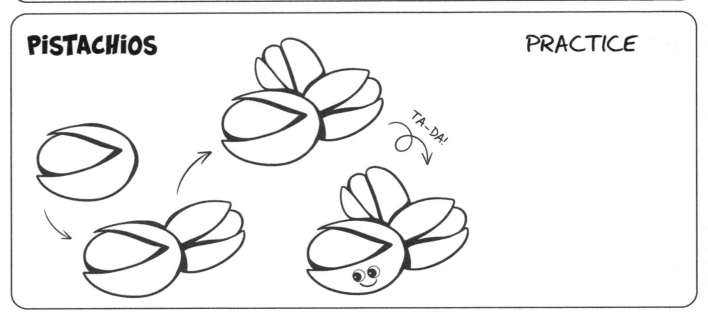

TA-DA!

TOMATO

TA-DA!

MUSHROOM

TA-DA!

CARROT

TA-DA!

RADISH

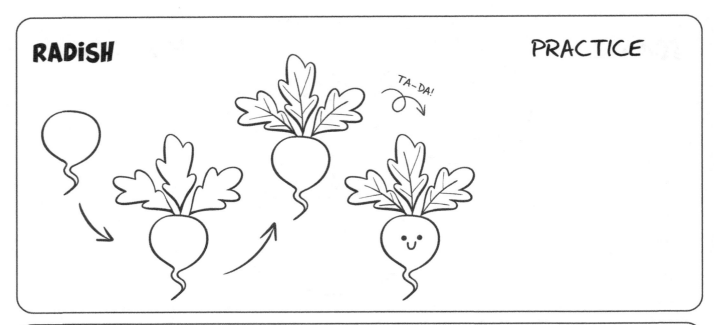

TA-DA!

BROCCOLI

TA-DA!

GARLIC BULB

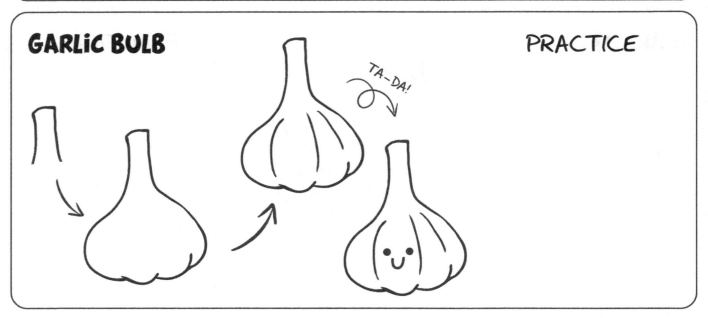

TA-DA!

ONION

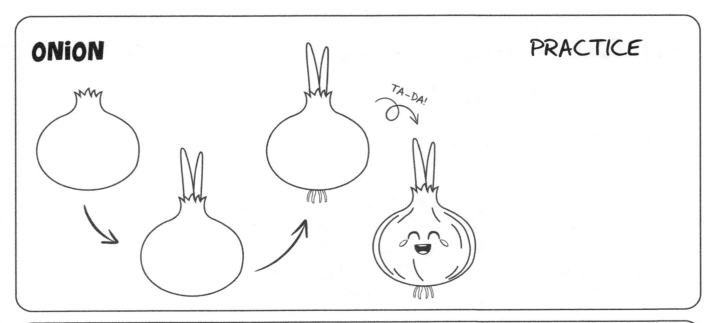

TA-DA!

LETTUCE

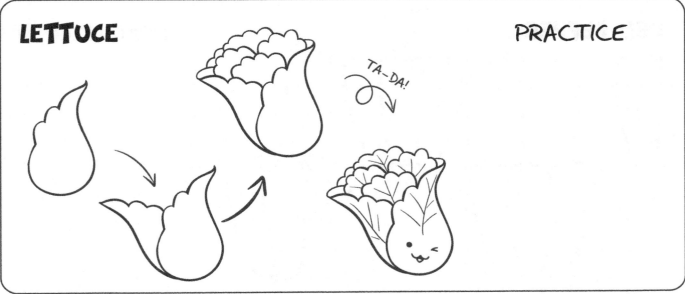

TA-DA!

EGGPLANT

TA-DA!

POTATOES

TA-DA!

BELL PEPPER

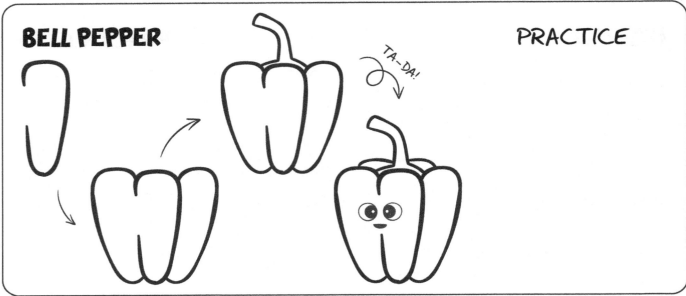

TA-DA!

KOHLRABI

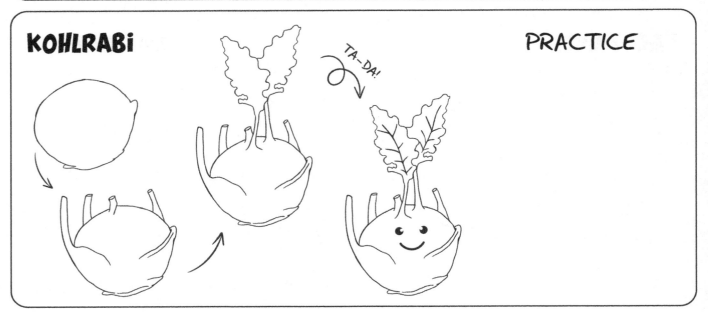

TA-DA!

ASPARAGUS

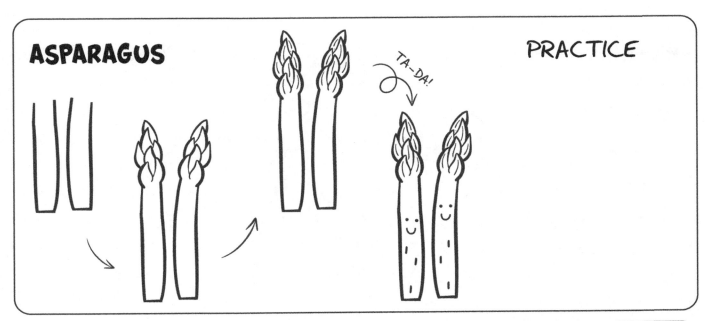

LEEK

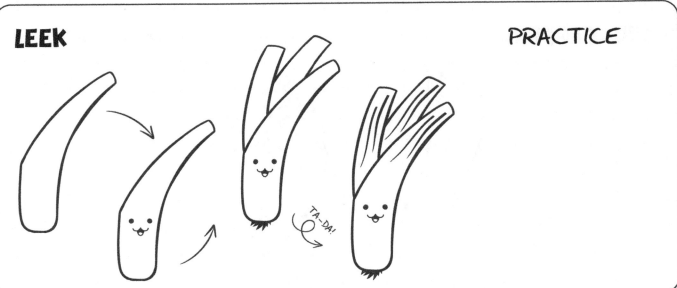

DAIKON

PEAS

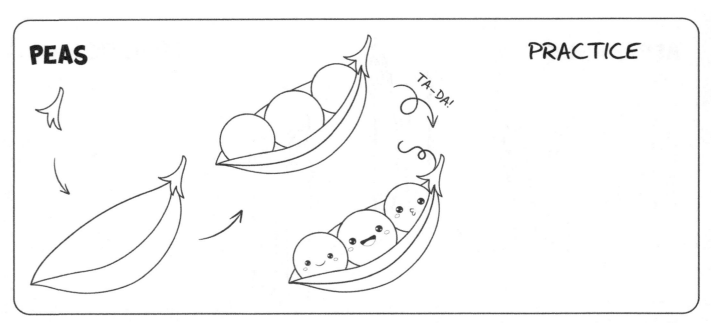

TA-DA!

CHILI PEPPER

TA-DA!

ZUCCHINI

TA-DA!

CORN

TA-DA!

ARTICHOKE

TA-DA!

CAULIFLOWER

TA-DA!

GINGER

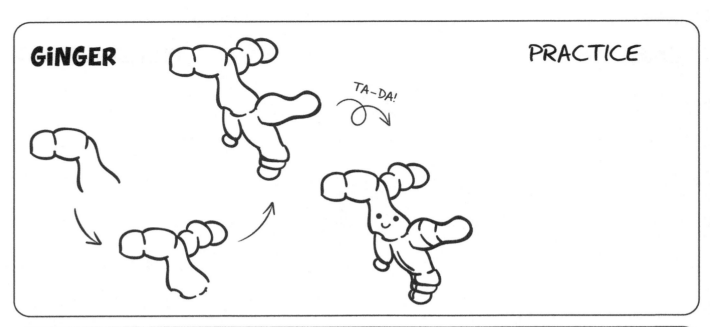

TA-DA!

CUCUMBERS

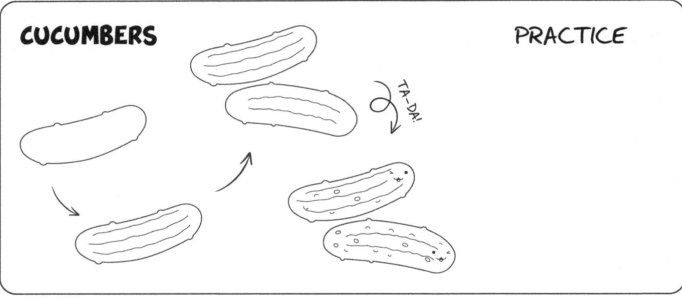

TA-DA!

SWEET POTATO

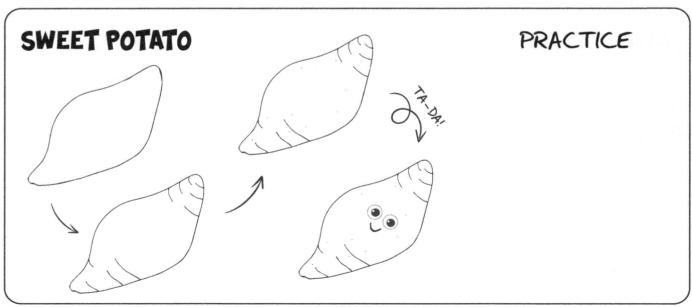

TA-DA!

ACORN PRACTICE

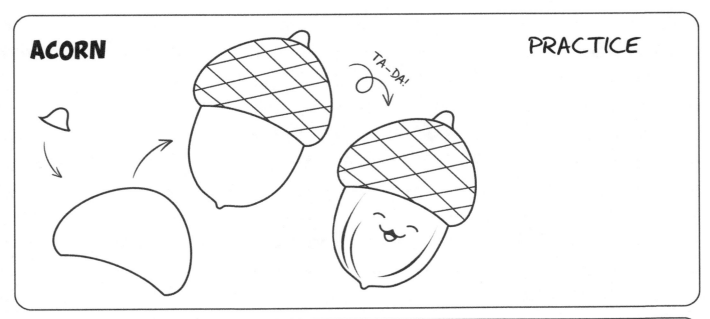

FENNEL PRACTICE

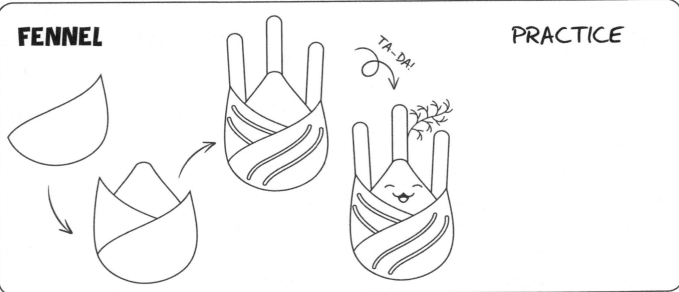

BUTTERNUT SQUASH PRACTICE

CACTUS

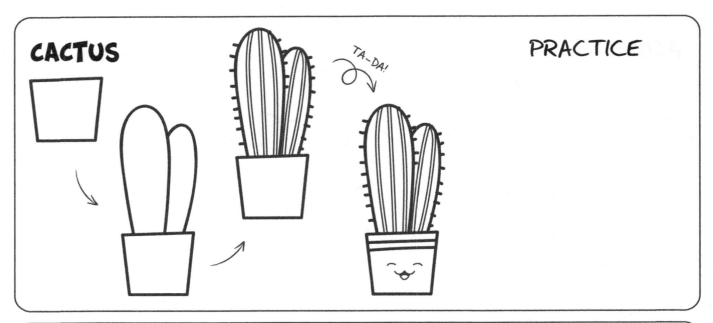

TA-DA!

TREE

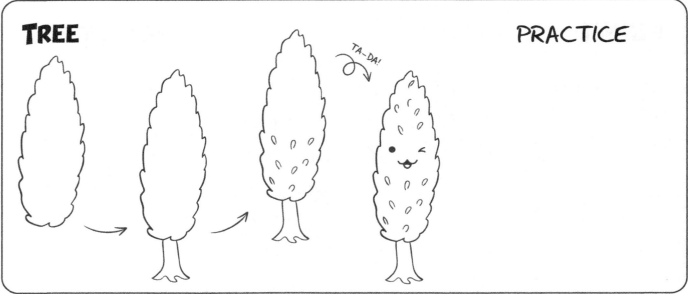

TA-DA!

LEAF

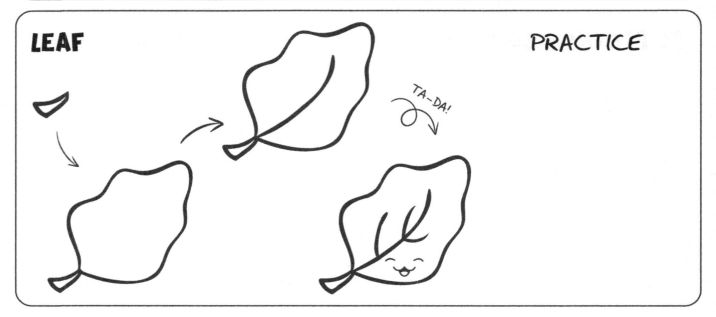

TA-DA!

HOLLY

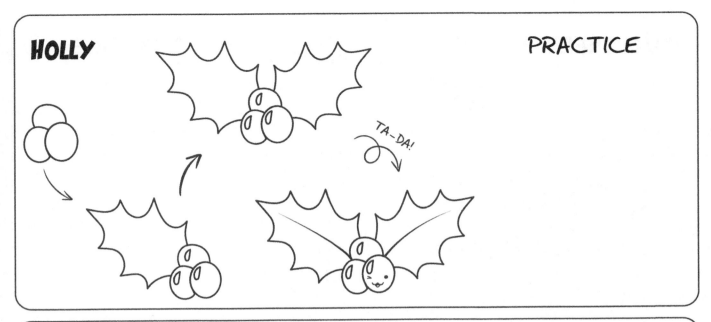

TA-DA!

CHRISTMAS TREE

TA-DA!

FLOWER

TA-DA!

PALM TREE

TA-DA!

TULIP

TA-DA!

BOUQUET

TA-DA!

BELLFLOWER

TA-DA!

GRASS BUSH

TA-DA!

WiLLOW BRANCH

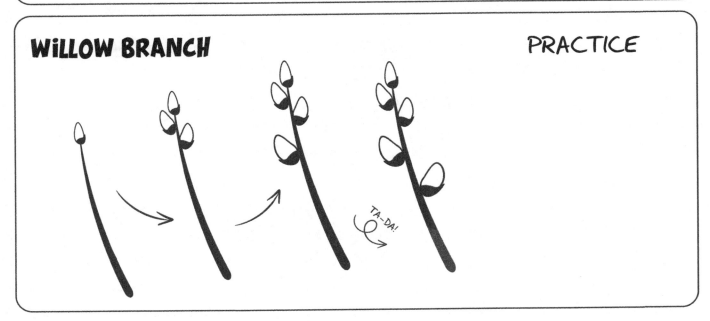

TA-DA!

ANIMALS AND EVERYDAY THINGS

DOG

DINOSAUR

CHICK

BEAR

BEE

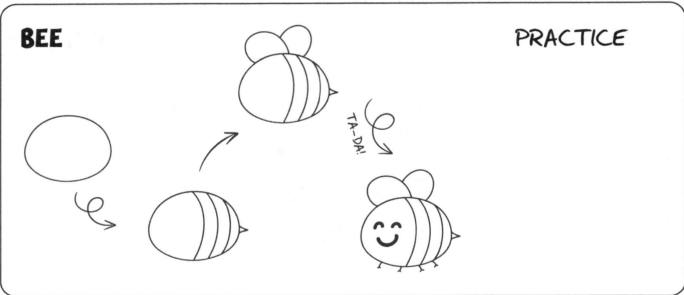

RABBiT

TIGER

RACCOON

MONKEY

SQUID

PENGUIN

SHEEP

GiRAFFE

TA-DA!

SQUiRREL

TA-DA!

ZEBRA

TA-DA!

FOX

POLAR BEAR

KOALA

LADYBUG

TA-DA!

EAGLE

TA-DA!

PiG

TA-DA!

iGUANA

LEOPARD

HEDGEHOG

FISH

TA-DA!

SCORPION

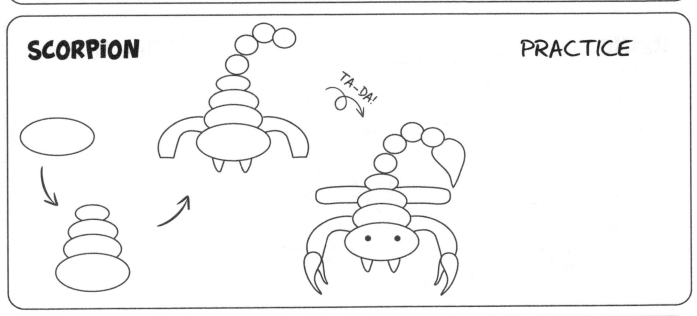

TA-DA!

HIPPO

TA-DA!

KANGAROO

RHINO

NARWHAL

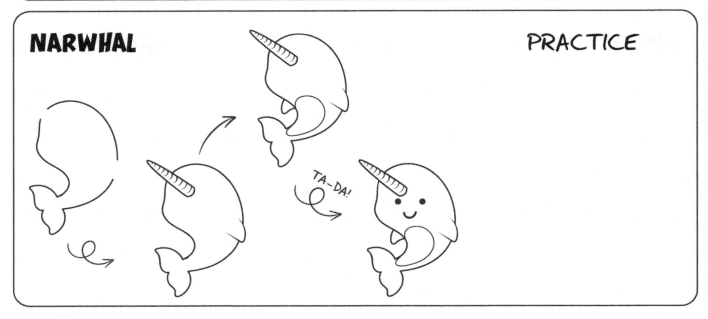

TURTLE

TA-DA!

CENTIPEDE

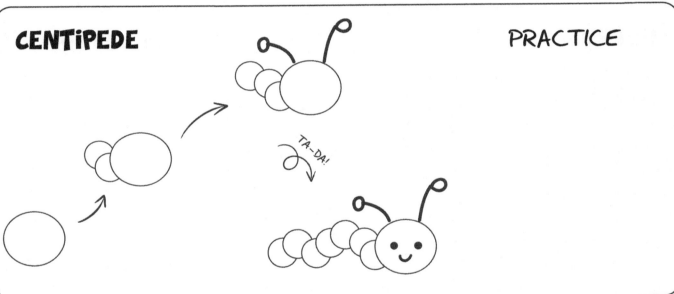

TA-DA!

SHARK

TA-DA!

MOUSE

PUPPY

FROG

HORSE

TA-DA!

DUCK

WHALE

TA-DA!

CROCODILE PRACTICE

OWL PRACTICE

ELEPHANT PRACTICE

CAT PRACTICE

HAMSTER PRACTICE

PANDA PRACTICE

DOLPHIN

TA-DA!

JELLYFISH

TA-DA!

SEAL

TA-DA!

SNAKE

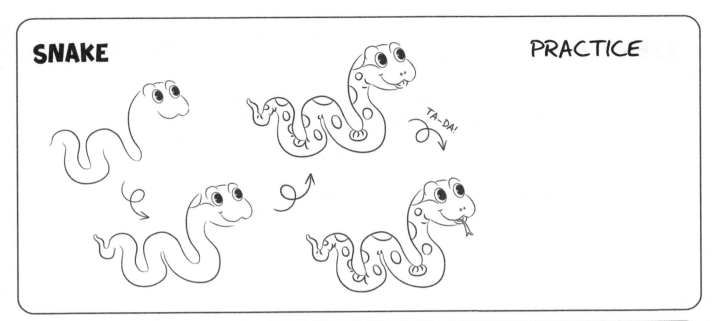

BUNNY

BUTTERFLY

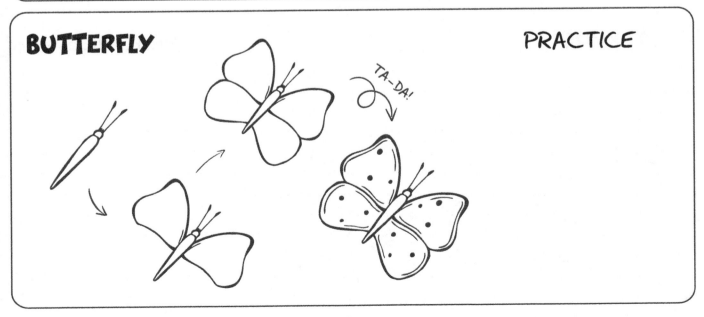

HYENA

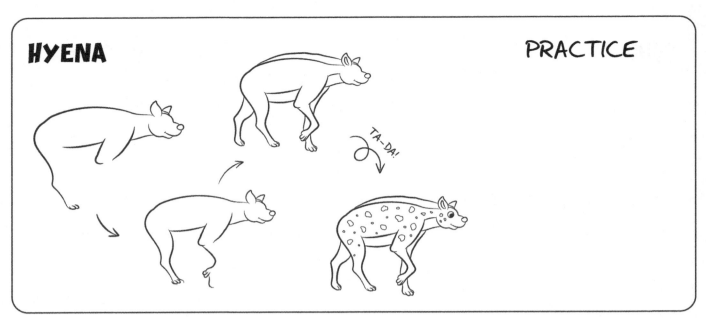

TA-DA!

ALLIGATOR

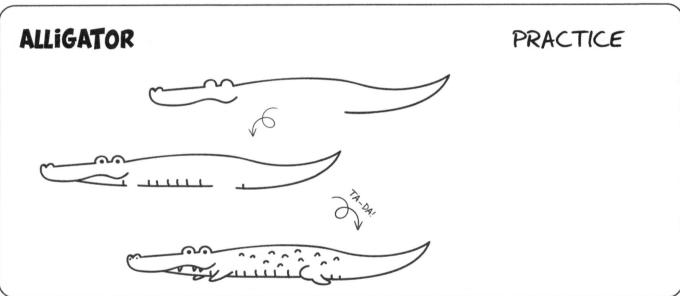

TA-DA!

PLATYPUS

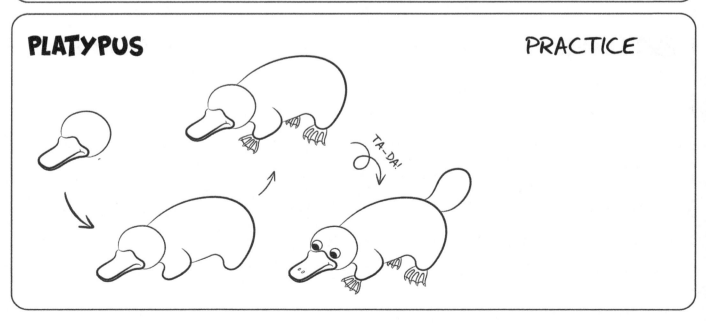

TA-DA!

SUN

TA-DA!

RAINBOW

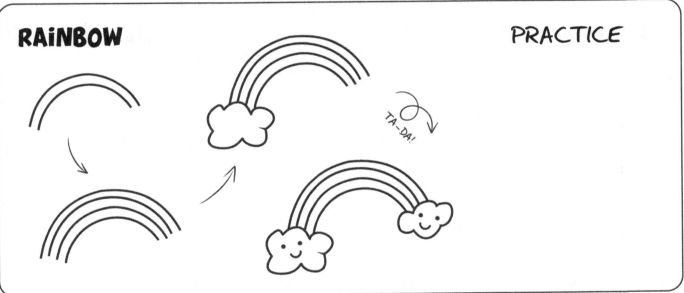

TA-DA!

JERRYCAN

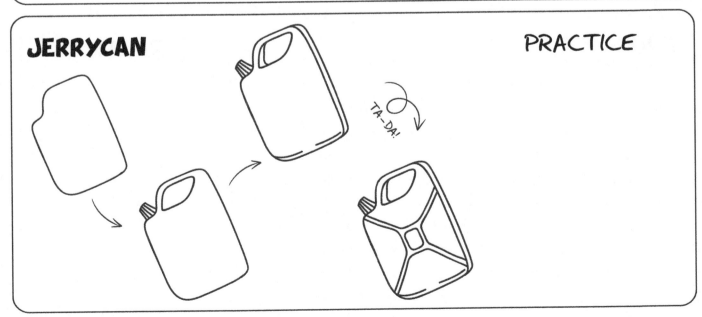

TA-DA!

TOILET PAPER

TA-DA!

LAPTOP

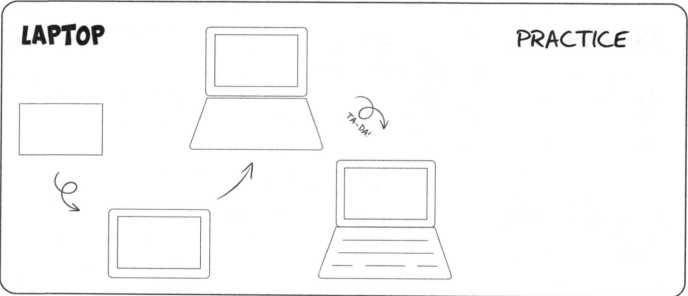

TA-DA!

BOOK

TA-DA!

CANDLE

SCREWDRIVER

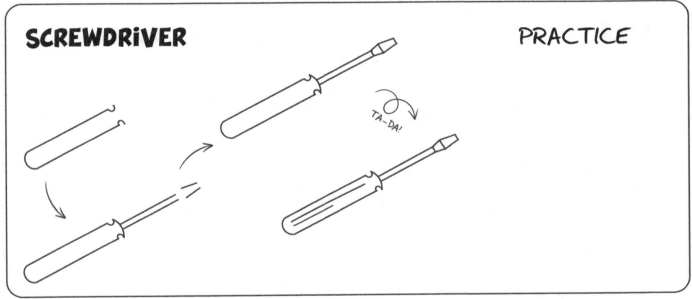

SAFETY HELMET

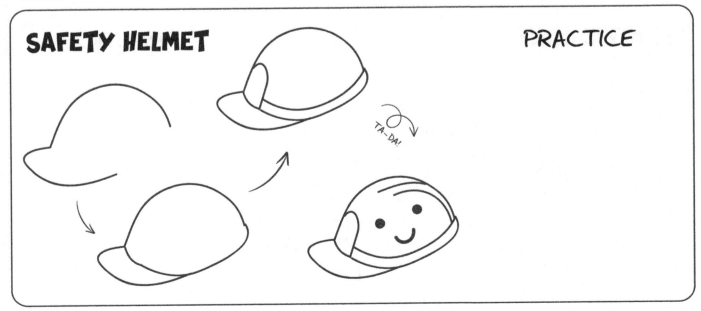

PLIERS

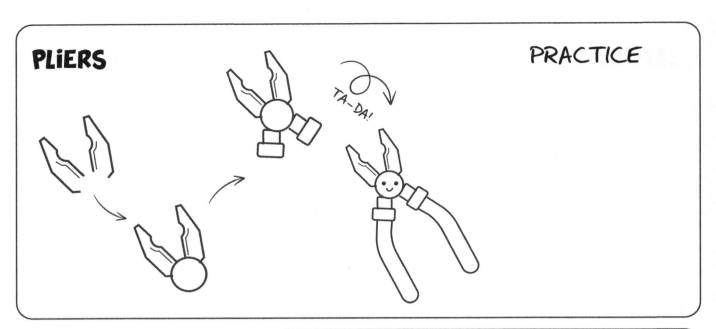

TA-DA!

PENCIL

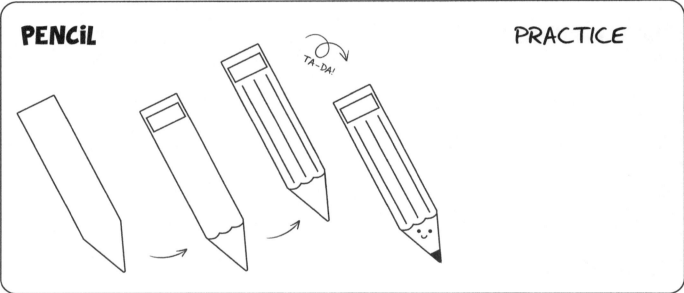

TA-DA!

TRAFFIC CONE

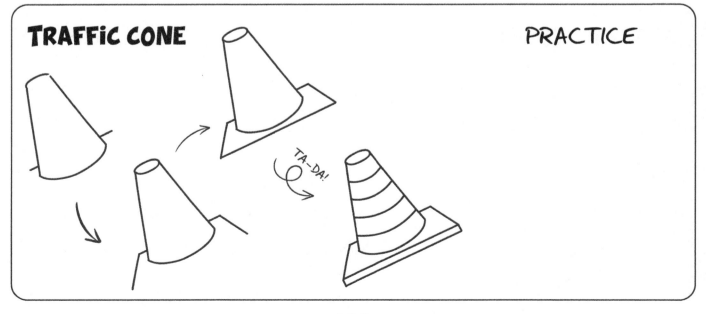

TA-DA!

SCREW

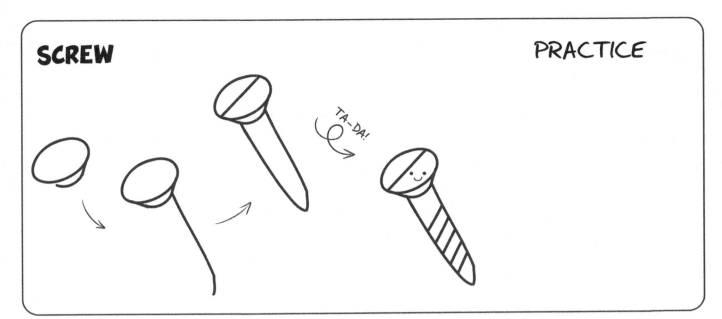

GiFT

DiAMOND

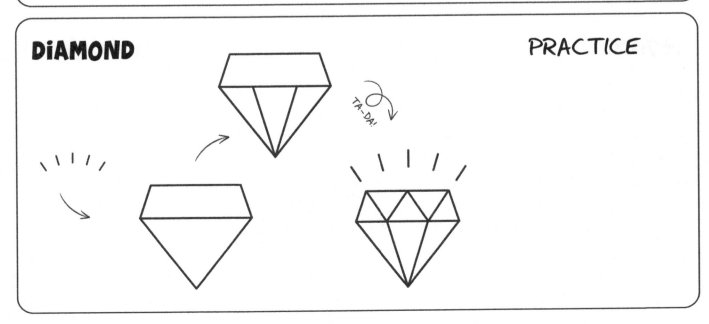

UMBRELLA

TA-DA!

TELEPHONE

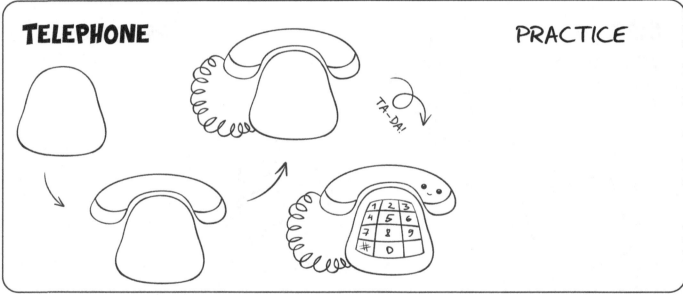

TA-DA!

MOON

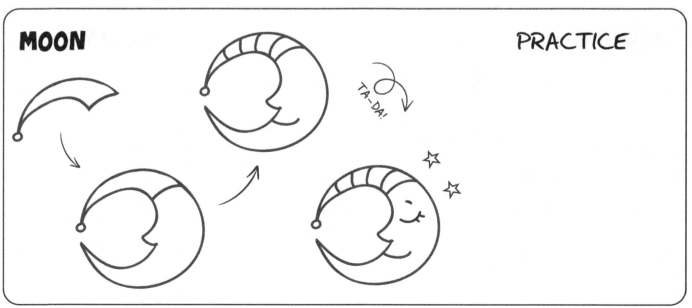

TA-DA!

Made in the USA
Coppell, TX
07 April 2024

30852335R00063